SPEAK

YOUR

VOICE

SPEAK
YOUR
VOICE

Unmute Your Voice.
Be Heard.
Get Your Power Back.

Dr. Sarah Renee Langley

SPEAK YOUR VOICE: Unmute Your Voice. Be Heard. Get Your Power Back. Copyright © 2018 by Dr. Sarah Renee Langley

All rights reserved. No part of this book may be reproduced, stored in a retrieval system, or transmitted in any form or by any means, electronic, mechanical, photocopying, recording, scanning, or otherwise, without the prior written permission of the publisher.

ISBN 978-0-9973341-2-8

Printed in the United States of America

DISCLAIMER

All the material contained in this book is provided for educational and informational purposes only. No responsibility can be taken for any results or outcomes resulting from the use of this material. While every attempt has been made to provide information that is both accurate and effective, the author does not assume any responsibility for the accuracy or use/misuse of this information.

DEDICATION

For Ma Jackson

Your Prayers and Perseverance
Propelled Me
To Finally
Speak My Voice

For My Mother Mary

Your voice has made me strong
Your hum now keeps me moving

For the Sheroes who shared their #MeToo Moments

Demonstrating courage, contribution, and commitment
by speaking your voices in this book.

FOR YOU

The Value And Worth Of Women Are Being Challenged Every Single Day, And It Gives More Courage, More Strength And More Determination To Stand Up, Solider Up, And Speak Up For The Purposeful And Powerful Pioneer That She Truly Is.

From worthless to priceless.
From life defining you to life refining you.
From thinking perfect is right to knowing being human is real.

Sarah Renee Langley
Sexual Assault Survivor And Activist
#speakyourvoice

CONTENTS

ACKNOWLEDGMENTS. 11
FOREWORD. 12
PREFACE 15
INTRODUCTION. 17
PURPOSE OF THIS BOOK 18
HOW TO USE THIS BOOK 20
SPEAK YOUR VOICE: TELL YOUR TRUTH 21
    MY NARRATIVE 22
    THE EDUCATION. 23
    THE CONVERSATION. 27
    THE REVELATION 30
    SELF REFLECTION EXERCISE 32
SEARCH YOUR VOICE: FIND YOURSELF 33
    MY NARRATIVE 34
    THE EDUCATION. 35
    THE CONVERSATION. 36
    THE REVELATION 40
    SELF REFLECTION EXERCISE 42
    INTERLUDE #1: SARAH, ME TOO 43
FIND YOUR VOICE: WHERE YOU LOSE IT. . . . 46
    MY NARRATIVE 47
    THE EDUCATION. 51
    THE CONVERSATION. 52

    THE REVELATION 57
    SELF REFLECTION EXERCISE 60
GET YOUR VOICE: GET YOUR OWN IDENTITY . . 61
    MY NARRATIVE 62
    THE EDUCATION. 68
    THE CONVERSATION. 70
    THE REVELATION 72
    SELF REFLECTION EXERCISE 74
    INTERLUDE #2: SARAH, ME TOO 75
BUILD YOUR VOICE: START FROM THE
BEGINNING 78
    MY NARRATIVE 79
    THE EDUCATION. 83
    THE CONVERSATION. 85
    THE REVELATION 88
    SELF REFLECTION EXERCISE 90
HEAR YOUR VOICE: LISTEN MORE TO YOUR
NEEDS 91
    MY NARRATIVE 92
    THE EDUCATION. 96
    THE CONVERSATION. 98
    THE REVELATION 100
    SELF REFLECTION EXERCISE 102
    INTERLUDE #3: SARAH, ME TOO 103
LOVE YOUR VOICE: EMBRACE YOU 106

    MY NARRATIVE 107
    THE EDUCATION. 113
    THE CONVERSATION. 116
    THE REVELATION 120
    SELF REFLECTION EXERCISE 122
SHOW YOUR VOICE: DEMONSTRATE. 123
    MY NARRATIVE 124
    THE EDUCATION. 128
    THE CONVERSATION. 134
    THE REVELATION 137
    SELF REFLECTION EXERCISE 138
OWN YOUR VOICE: CLAIM IT! POWER 139
    MY NARRATIVE 140
    THE EDUCATION. 141
    THE CONVERSATION. 143
    THE REVELATION 144
    SELF REFLECTION EXERCISE 146
    INTERLUDE #4: SARAH, ME TOO 147
BE YOUR VOICE: YOU AND YOUR VOICE BECOMES ONE. 148
    MY NARRATIVE 149
    THE EDUCATION. 151
    THE CONVERSATION. 155
    THE REVELATION 159
    SELF REFLECTION EXERCISE 162

GIVE YOUR VOICE: GIVE BACK 163
    MY NARRATIVE 164
    THE EDUCATION. 167
    THE CONVERSATION. 169
    THE REVELATION 173
    SELF REFLECTION EXERCISE 175
    INTERLUDE #5: SARAH, ME TOO 176
SHARE YOUR VOICE: THAT'S YOUR RESPONSIBILITY. 177
    MY NARRATIVE 178
    THE EDUCATION. 186
    THE CONVERSATION. 188
    THE REVELATION 199
SELL YOUR VOICE: ROCK YOUR VOICE 202
    YOUR NARRATIVE. 203
    THE EDUCATION. 203
    THE CONVERSATION. 205
    THE REVELATION 207
    SELF REFLECTION EXERCISE 209
CONCLUSION 210
AFTERWORD 211
RESOURCE: ROCK YOUR VOICE ....,.... 214
BUILD YOUR MESSAGE FOR MILLIONS 215
ABOUT THE AUTHOR. 218

SPEAK YOUR VOICE

ACKNOWLEDGMENTS

I want to thank All of the courageous Sheroes and Heroes who decided to speak their voices. You are the reason. You made this book possible. You inspire me.

I want to acknowledge the Unsung Sheroes and Heroes who may be suffering in silence because their offenders were not celebrities that could get their stories out into the limelight. This book will.

I also want to acknowledge my counsel, committee, those who helped me edit this book, and those sharing this book with the world so that we all get into position to Speak Our Voices.

I want to acknowledge the movements like #metoo and #timesup and countless other initiatives that dared to disrupt and interrupt the patterns and cycles we have been used to for far too long.

Thanks to the readers who were drawn to read this book and decided to become and remain the Victor over their lives.

Lastly, I want to thank my mother, the one who is without a voice, for always teaching and demonstrating how to speak my voice. And my daddy, who forever (I do say this in love) keeps me raising my voice. Daily. I love you both.

FOREWORD

Not to be outwitted by Google, the famed Webster's dictionary defines "voice" as "the expression of something in words." An expression is the outward exhalation of something that is inside yearning to get out.

My initial encounter with Ms. Langley was in a business context where the masks hiding expression were in full effect. However, I knew that there was a kinship with Ms. Langley that breached the surface of our cursory interaction. I sensed a deeper resonance. There had to be. Ms. Langley reached out to me some time ago to assist in the planning for the *Speak Your Voice* book project and movement. Bubbling below the surface was the kinship that I knew was there all along.

Once we got beyond the lady-like chit-chat and polite small talk, it became clear that Ms. Langley's life's work was to take up the mantle for womenfolk. Her book *Speak Your Voice* is evidence of this mantle. Through the candor and transparency of *Speak Your Voice,* Ms. Langley takes us on a familiarly painful journey of self-discovery and the power of enlightenment. Ms. Langley writes:

". . . I remember him putting his hands over my mouth. That was truly my first experience of having my voice silenced, having my voice muted, having my voice unheard..."

. . . "Voice unheard" - the realization that we have all had events in our lives that have inevitably silenced our voices both physically and psychological is very transformative. The tangential reality is that sometimes even the loudest screams can go unheard. Standing in the bosom of those realities is Ms. Langley's willingness to bear her soul to give voice to the voiceless. As a juxtaposition to the notables of the current *#MeToo* movement, Ms. Langley gives voice to women who are not famous or wealthy and who have had experiences with oppressors who are not famous or wealthy. All voices matter. All voices should be heard.

Undoubtedly, there may be a feeling for some that they are not worthy of giving public voice to their private pain. However, Ms. Langley takes us through her personal journey in overcoming self-doubt and allows us to take aim at our own self-doubt. This self-doubt is embodied in our ability to put on a front in public and appear to be doing "just fine"; while suffering alone in private. Maya Angelou in her adaptation of *Paul Laurence Dunbar's, We Wear the Mask* opined that:

> *We smile but oh my God*
>   *Our tears to thee from tortured souls arise*
>   *And we sing Oh Babydoll, now we sing…*
> *The clay is vile beneath our feet*
> *And long the mile*
> *But let the world think otherwise.*
> *We wear the mask.*

Through the pages of *Speak Your Voice*, I challenge you to drop any proverbial masks you may have and join the movement.

Sarah Renee Langley

Sarah Renee Langley has lived this story. She is fully aware that by sharing her truth it connects her to all those sticky perils of the human experience – rejection, abandonment, security, hope, and desire ending with self-realization, exhalation, and liberation. So, saddle up and lock arms with Ms. Langley in her journey towards giving full voice to her personal pain – out loud and unapologetically.

Through the sisterhood of the *Speak Your Voice* movement, Sarah Renee Langley will guide you along the path towards sloughing off some of your pains. This is your time, this is your moment, this is your movement.

Speak Your Voice.

By Aurelia Durant, Esq.

SPEAK YOUR VOICE

PREFACE

During the 2016 Presidential Race in the United States of America, about 54% of women voted for Hillary Clinton, who eventually lost to Donald Trump. An estimated 52% of White Women voted for Trump.

What was Former First Lady Michelle Obama's reaction to this? The New York Times reported Mrs. Obama as saying,

"Quite frankly we saw this in this election. As far as I'm concerned, any woman who voted against Hillary Clinton voted against their own voice in a way... What does it mean for us as women? That we look at those two candidates, as women, and many of us said, 'That guy. He's better for me. His voice is more true to me.' Well, to me that just says you don't like your voice. You like the thing we're told to like."

Bingo. A defining moment for me. This was a turning point that had me do what is a called pattern interrupt. I was literally interrupting my own usual and customary thought patterns with questions like, "What do I think about my voice?" (for the record I did not vote for Trump). "What does this all mean regarding my voice?" Everyone is blessed with their own voices, but there is much to be explored about our voices that we need to unlock so that we can harness our strength not only for our good but for the good of others, too. Do we even understand our own voices? Are we aware of the power that lies within it? Do we know of that power and are just too afraid of it?

Marianne Williamson's Our Deepest Fear suggests that we need to stop playing small, as it serves no one. We need to no longer be afraid of our light, but to instead use our light to achieve greatness for ourselves, and to also set examples for others who are watching our light shine so that others know it is OK to shine their light as well.

    We need no longer curse the darkness, but to be the light and shine for others. We can also use our light as a way to Search Our Voices, Find Our Voices, Get Our Voices, Build Our Voices, Hear Our Voices, Love Our Voices, Show Our Voices, Own Our Voices, Be Our Voices, Give Our Voices, and ultimately, Share Our Voices. We are obligated to Speak Our Voices so that others can be set free from their own darkness as we also get set free when we Speak. Our. Voice.

Speak Your Voice.

Unmute Your Voice.

Be Heard.

Get Your Power Back.

Now.

INTRODUCTION

As I write this book, so many flashbacks have come, so many thoughts have run through my mind, so many emotions have resurfaced. But because you are in mind, I forced my fingers to the keyboard to speak my voice.

The problem is that at one point, I was not speaking my voice. I was very muted. I felt very empty, sometimes lifeless. Sometimes I would escape my own body. One thing that was terrible to me in the whole matter of having my voice silenced and not being heard was *disrespect*. It comes at a price when you have been violated, and you have chosen to cover it, not say anything about it, suffer with it for years, or do whatever you had to do to survive, feeling like no one cares or even knows what you've experienced. For me, it also translated into feeling insignificant, feeling very small, feeling like I was nothing. Yet, I can look back and see all the accomplishments I have made over the years despite what has happened to me. I can look back and be proud of how I was able to renew my shine, reclaim my time, and restore my voice. I learned how to be free to speak my voice. I had to because you were in my heart the entire time waiting for me to speak my voice. This is why we experience what we do so that others can hear our voices and learn from our life lessons, to obtain the hope, promise, and solutions shared to become overcomers. Powerful people ask powerful questions. Therefore, who is in your heart waiting for you to both get out of your way and theirs, show up and show out, and speak your voice?

There's nothing I want more than for you to Speak Your Voice. *Your Voice and Message Matters.*

PURPOSE OF THIS BOOK

The purpose of this book is to empower you to speak your voice, to know that you are important, that you are someone, that you have significant value, and that you have something worth listening to. I want to play a part in setting you free, to provide a safe space and a platform for your voice to be heard. But most importantly, I want to help strengthen you to take your freedom to another level. My hope for you is to experience and discover your greatness, no longer be held captive. You are to no longer be kept bound to your past, your challenges, or unfortunate tragedies that once silenced your voice.

Speak Your Voice is more than just a book. It's an initiative. It's your breakthrough. The Merriam-Webster Dictionary defines *breakthrough* as "warfare," "an act or instance of moving through or beyond an obstacle," "a person's first notable success," and "a sudden advance especially in knowledge and technique." *Speak Your Voice,* then, is about you waging war against the bondage that has enslaved you, being victorious in your press, reclaiming what was stolen from you, and helping other captives be set free through you speaking your voice.

Simply put, this book is intended to evoke education, conversation, and revelation in eight ways:

1. Educate everyone about signs and precursors to matters that can result in trauma and victimization so that we can be proactive and preventative rather than be reactive and constantly do damage control on such matters.

2. Start the conversation about the injustices and unfairness that result in trauma and victimization to raise awareness, evoke courage to speak out, and to develop an intolerance for inappropriate and unwelcomed behavior.
3. Reveal to you that you are not a victim but you are a victor and an overcomer over any and every obstacle you face.
4. Help you to no longer rob the world of your greatness because of what may have happened to you, but to turn this obstacle into an opportunity for you to speak your voice to those who need it.
5. Accept and embrace the fact that everything you go through develops into life lessons and tips and strategies to win at life, and to help others win as well through your life lessons.
6. Become. To become who you were purposed and designed to be. Not to succumb to the pain you have endured along the way, but to overcome and triumph over your trials and tribulations in life.
7. Create a legacy of speaking your voice so that others will do the same.
8. Contribute to others' breakthroughs through your message and story.

This is your defining moment to move through your obstacles, get courageous, be a disrupter in the world, look fear square in the face and do the very thing you thought you could not do, and that is to *Speak Your Voice Now*. Because the world awaits your voice.

HOW TO USE THIS BOOK

Use this book as an opportunity to learn how to speak your voice for your breakthrough. As you reflect and answer the questions that are at the end of each chapter, do not look at what *you became* as a result of your situation or incident, but rather reframe, which means look at the situation differently, and then realize what you *can become* as a result of your situation or incident.

Why? Because setbacks are merely opportunities for comebacks, and this is your comeback moment!

Respect your slots, which means, look at the time on your calendar and pen yourself in for about 30 minutes a day for reading this book and doing the self-reflective exercises at the end of each chapter that will position you to speak your voice.

This book will help you learn how to use the power of your voice to self-actualize, build your character and confidence, and even learn how to leverage and monetize your message to make a significant impact in the lives you are to serve while earning a substantial income. This bonus chapter is my gift to you. I guarantee that after reading, you will consider speaking your voice as a career. You will discover how people are waiting to pay you top dollar for your story and message of hope, promise, breakthrough, transformation, liberation, and freedom.

My only asks are that you raise the standard, break your silence, get your breakthrough and own your greatness. It is time for you to walk in your purpose, claim your power and even generate profit along the way (I am always the business coach). Limitless LeadHER, it is time to *Speak Your Voice.*

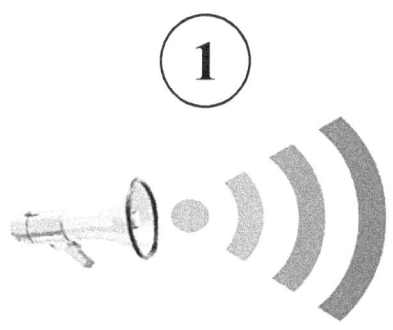

SPEAK YOUR VOICE

TELL YOUR TRUTH

"My silences had not protected me. Your silence will not protect you. But for every real word spoken, for every attempt I had ever made to speak those truths for which I am still seeking, I had made contact with other women while we examined the words to fit a world in which we all believed, bridging our differences."

--Audre Lorde

Sarah Renee Langley

MY NARRATIVE

No. I was not in the hotel room with Bill Cosby taking Quaaludes to relax me.

No. I was not sitting on the casting couch with Harvey Weinstein giving the best dictation and audition of my life.

No. I was not in Matt Lauer's office with him alone when the door automatically locked behind me like I was being sealed in a vault of some sort.

No. I wasn't in the studio when Charlie Rose's naked @$$ paraded around to get my attention as if his "goods" were appalling, I mean, appealing or alluring.

Actually, I was an 18-year-old young woman literally about to leave for college when the unthinkable happened to me. He wasn't a celebrity, a political figure or a beloved thought leader, just a 'regular' boy from the neighborhood, whom I trusted as a friend. He called me on the day I was leaving for college and asked me to come to his house to pick up the "going away gift" he had for me.

I didn't feel any unease at his request because he is my friend. My parents were already waiting in the car to take me to the university, so they could wait a few minutes more.

I hurried down to his house. He greeted me at the door and told me that the gift was upstairs in his room and for me to go up and get it. "Ok, no problem," I thought to myself as he followed me up the stairs. When I arrived at his room and didn't see a gift in sight, I barely had a chance to turn around and ask where the gift was before he pushed me to the bed, forced his hand over my mouth, pinned me down, and raped me.

That unknown raped this unknown.

Minutes felt like hours. Days. Years. Infinity.

I died that day. As he lifted from off of me, dripping from his penis, I asked, "Am I still a virgin?" "Well, technically, yeah," he replied, probably to put both of us at ease from what had just happened. But I didn't believe him. I was bewildered and felt lost in my own body. I associated my identity with my virginity. I couldn't believe what he had done to me. I trusted him. Now he is a liar. I totally disengaged from myself and dissociated from everything else. I had to because I could not bear giving my parents any reason to suspect something went wrong at his house once I got in the car to go to the university.

So yeah. #metoo.

THE EDUCATION

SEXUAL ASSAULT, HARASSMENT, AND MISCONDUCT

It has not always been clear as to what sexual assault really is, but it has been talked about more recently due to the multiple allegations against celebrities in Hollywood like producer Harvey Weinstein, and actor, Kevin Spacey, House of Cards.

According to the United States Department of Justice,

sexual assault is "any type of sexual contact or behavior that occurs without the explicit consent of the recipient." In essence, sexual assault is a term used to describe a group of behaviors or activities that are sexual such as fondling, rape attempt, or rape itself.

Sexual assault is not solely the sexual act, but is when a person coerces, forces or manipulates another person to engage in sexual activity against their own will or without their consent. It is also seen as subtler and covert behaviors like creating an unconducive environment, suggestive jokes, comments, looks or even body languages that sexually arouses the offender. It starts with the offender's thought, belief and value system regarding gender, race and sexual orientation. It then escalates to verbal expressions such as jokes, comments, and inappropriate touching. Unfortunately, it escalates to sexual assault. Though every victim's experience is quite unique, they can be grouped into different types. Interestingly, the most commonly known type of assault is stranger assault. However, studies have shown that 86% of victims know their perpetrator, which classifies either acquaintance/date rape or intimate partner sexual assault.

According to U.S. Equal Employment Opportunity Commission, also known as the EEOC, Sexual Harassment "is a form of sexual discrimination that violates the Civil Rights Act of 1964". The EEOC further states that forms of Sexual harassment include unwelcome sexual advances, requests, favors, and other verbal and physical sexual conduct that affects their individual unemployment, work performance, and overall work environment. Insights West reported that 22% of the participants of their study stated they were humiliated or offended by sexual conduct, comment or contact in the workplace. Twenty-eight percent stated that the sexual conduct comment or contact was associated with conditions of their employment or promotion. Sexual harassment can start with unwanted behaviors, like comments, text messages, jokes, and pictures. It then escalates to rubbing against someone, kissing, and inappropriate touching, to ultimately escalating to sexual assault. Unfortunately, anybody can be a victim of sexual assault, and it can happen anywhere or at any time. It has no age restriction, gender bias, disability favors, or even socio- economic boundaries.

Sexual Misconduct is classified as unwelcomed sexual behavior that is committed by force, manipulation, or coercion without consent. It is important to note that there are varying degrees to sexual misconduct, and it can occur between strangers, acquaintances, and by those involved in an intimate, sexual relationship. Examples of sexual misconduct includes sexual assault, sexual harassment, sexual exploitation, and sexual intimidation.

What is the history of sexual assault, harassment, and misconduct? It all started way before Anita Hill and Clarence Thomas. It is interesting that to date, there are varying definitions coupled with people's opinions and experiences regarding sexual assault, harassment, and misconduct. The challenge becomes the court of public opinion that weighs in if someone is sexually assaulted, harassed, or inappropriately touched. Unfortunately, we have a considerable amount of women bashing, shaming, and condemning women who speak their voices about such heinous acts like sexual misconduct. From minimizing perpetrators' behaviors to misplacing accountability onto the victims, it is ever a wonder why we are confused and still green at how to handle such cases.

In the U.S., women in the 20th century suffered in silence while enduring mistreatment in the workplace without any security or solutions, other than quit. Sexual harassment was coined in 1975 by a group of women at Cornell University when a former employee applied for unemployment benefits due to her boss sexually harassing her. She was denied, and it was on from there. By 1977, it was confirmed that women can *sue* employers for sexual harassment under the 1964 Civil Right Act. In 1992, harassment complaints filed with the Equal Employment Opportunity Commission went up 50% since Congress passed the law for victims to sue for sexual harassment. And now the fight for workplace equality and women's rights continues.

The effects of sexual assault are in diverse forms, some lasting a relatively short time, while others last a lifetime. It is noteworthy that both men and women experience sexual assault and its traumatic effects, though it is far more prevalent in women. Physical effects include bruises, bleeding, and soreness, while physiological effects include involuntary shaking and sexual dysfunction. Emotional effects of sexual assault include fear, anger, blame, and helplessness while the social effects include shame, guilt, mistrust, and denial.

Common psychological effects of sexual assault are trauma, in particular, Post-traumatic stress disorder, also known as PTSD. Symptoms of PTSD include flashbacks, nightmares, severe anxiety and uncontrollable thoughts. Further trauma to any form of sexual assault, harassment and misconduct include depression, suicidal thoughts, and attempts. Additionally, Dissociation is an unconscious process that protects one from unacceptable painful memories to cope. Other symptoms include body memories that result in psychosomatic or body symptoms that doctors cannot explain, like headaches, stomach problems, and dizziness. Have you experienced any of these symptoms? Are you no longer affected? Have you overcome these traumatic effects? If not, how do you cope? What are you doing about it? Let's have a conversation.

THE CONVERSATION

LIFE LESSONS

I share my story with you in mind. Not for sympathy, fame, or book deals. Conversely, it's to simply speak my voice. The women and men who courageously spoke out against the outrage of big-named people struck a chord deep down inside, birthing this initiative, this Speak Your Voice Initiative. This initiative is for the unknowns like me who have suffered, and who continually suffer in silence. I want to speak my voice for the unsung sheroes and heroes whom their perpetrators are unknowns, like the one who raped me. These women and men need a platform and an opportunity to unmute their voices, be heard, and get their power back.

As an American country, we vehemently defend our first amendment and constitutional right to freedom of speech, until it is unacceptable to call out the TRUTH. What is truth anyway? The Oxford English Dictionary defines truth as "that which is true or by fact or reality." What determines facts and reality is our perception of what is right. It is time to speak your truth.

With the flurry of #metoo stories surfacing, our current times are revealing just how unstable many of our relationships, both personal and professional, are as they occur in critical places of trust. And as a result, we walk around with masks on. I talk about the 3 Masks we wear in my book, It's Your Turn NOW! 7 Secrets To Living Life On Your Own Terms, with the mini downloadable version made available to you for free at www.drsarahreneelangley.com. We looked polished on the outside but fractured and bankrupted on the inside. At our expenses, we have harbored secrets of what has happened to us, all the while excusing our violators to repeatedly offend other innocent victims. We became imposters, not living a truly authentic life, and for what? For broken promises, hopes, and dreams that they fed us? For fame and fortune? For love? For Power? To avoid pain, shame, or being blackballed? Couldn't we just get a job at McDonald's or at our cousin's cleaners if we were kicked out of the limelight?

Thanks, Eddie Murphy, for those Delirious days.

SPEAK YOUR VOICE

Seriously, what does that say about our own self-love? Perhaps it's none of the above that's the answer. We keep secrets because we do not want to be revictimized. Our society unwittingly puts the victim on trial surrounding the actual events leading to the assault or harassment or misconduct. In fact, Motivational guru, Tony Robbins caught flack at his event for sharing his sentiments regarding the #Metoo Movement, citing that those who are part of the movement are calling out their abusers and *"destroying these males"* and *"using significance as a drug"* to make themselves feel good. Robbins seems to state that those who are part of the movement perpetuate victimhood and cease not to stay liberated and free from their perpetrators of sexual abuse and harassment. One damning comment was when Robbins spoke of men he knows who choose not to hire qualified women to their companies because of fear of being accused of sexual assault or harassment. *Yeah, he tried it,* until Twitter set him straight. He has since apologized for the *misunderstanding* of his comments and that he commits to "being part of the solution" to help "educate others so that we all stay true to the ideals of the #Metoo Movement."

Right.

No More! No more can these apparent state of thoughts and affairs carry on in this world. It cannot happen from the White House to God's House any longer. We cannot give freedom to the wrong people. I am astonished at how the list of accusers grows. Why am I so mad at this situation?

My babies. No, I am not pregnant with Louis C.K.'s babies. I am not a mother yet, and I decided to Speak My Voice for their chance to be born in a world where the difference between good touch/bad touch and what's appropriate and what's not appropriate is crystal clear. I want my children and your children, grandchildren, and great-grandchildren to live in a world where ownership, responsibility, and accountability are delegated to the appropriate parties, not displaced to the victims. May our future live in a world where moral compasses, values, and mutual respect trumps entitlement, immaturity, and lust for dominance and control.

I choose to play my part in moving the needle forward in empowering you and others to become who you are born to be, optimize in your greatness, and be the most significant contributor to making this world a better place because our roles on this earth are bigger, beautiful and beyond us. It is time to Speak Our Voices.

THE REVELATION

TIPS AND RECOMMENDATIONS

Napoleon Hill said, "The key to success is the pursuit of knowledge." I will add to this sentence, "The key to success is the pursuit of knowledge…of who you are."

You are on the road to learning who you are to become as a result of what you have gone through. It is a matter of shifting your mindset and level of consciousness to that which will inevitably serve you and others well. Here are some tips and recommendations I have learned along the way for you to implement:

- ✓ **Accept** that your past is not your future. It is a vehicle that produces your life lessons. Learn from your past and use it to your advantage to help others
- ✓ **Focus on becoming**! What makes us happy isn't about what we get but what we become. Today, you are not fully who you are, but you are on a journey to self-actualization, which, simply put, means you are becoming the best version of yourself.
- ✓ **Focus on contribution.** You do have much to offer in this world if you just get out of your own way to see it. Ask yourself, what can you give today to move the vision forward in making this world a better place.
- ✓ **Recognize** and change any limiting beliefs about yourself, the world and of others.
- ✓ **Learn** aall that yyou can about yourself through self-reflection and by asking those you trust to describe you in one word. This is where you will start to pinpoint your purpose in life so you can have a plan of action to operating in your purpose.

These 5 tips and recommendations will help ignite your certainty and confidence to speak your voice and share with others your life lessons and tips and recommendations by helping others inevitably speak their voices.

SELF REFLECTION EXERCISE

To **SPEAK** Your Voice, get into a quiet space, and give yourself 15-30 minutes to do this exercise. Reflect, free associate, and write down your first thoughts that come to mind when answering the questions below without questioning or altering your answers.

What has been your narrative? What are your unspoken rules you live by to date?

_____
_____
_____

List all possible desires you have had in your heart since you were little.

_____
_____
_____

Categorize the top 3 desires and see if you are currently doing one of them. If not, why? If so, do you enjoy it?

_____
_____
_____

What kept you from fulfilling your desires? And what is the one thing you will do differently to fulfill them?

_____
_____
_____

SPEAK YOUR VOICE

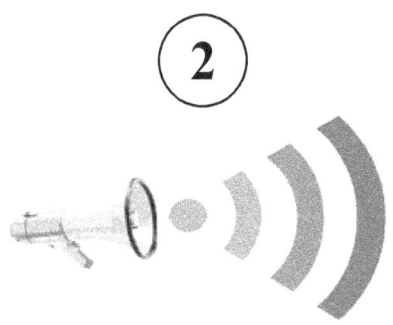

SEARCH YOUR VOICE
FIND YOURSELF

"Sometimes you find yourself in the middle of nowhere, and sometimes, in the middle of nowhere, you find yourself".

– LOVE-TIMAAJ.TUMBLR

Sarah Renee Langley

MY NARRATIVE

Upon entering the room, I only saw a bed, an open window, and a fan. I did not see a gift. When I turned around to ask the question – "Well, where's the gift? I need to hurry up and get to the car" – my friend pushed me to the bed, forced his hand over my mouth, pinned me to the bed as he pulled my pants down, and *raped me.*

It happened so fast, I could not believe it. I did not see this coming whatsoever. It was like I had an out-of-body experience. I mentally checked out; my brain could not fathom what was going on. When he ejaculated and pulled out, I watched him as he looked down at his member, dripping. Still, in shock, the only question I had for him was, "'Am I still a virgin?" Let me share why I asked that question. My identity was wrapped up in my virginity. I took pride in being one of the very few young girls in my neighborhood refraining from sex until marriage because of my Christian morals.

His response to me was, "Well, technically, yeah." Perhaps he said that because he must have seen the shock on my face and realized what he had just done. Indeed, he 'won' that day (I'll share the details of the infamous 'wager' later) while I died that day. I realized Mom and Dad were waiting in the car, and before they start looking for me, I would only have a few minutes to get myself together, wipe myself off, straighten up my clothes, get out of his house, hurry to the car, and pretend as if nothing had ever happened. Yes, it means I had to bury the entire encounter along with me in it.

In an instant, all that my parents taught me about being important, significant, and having a voice vanished in a matter of minutes. The "I got a gift for you" experience showed me that I was insignificant, worthless and voiceless. He muted my voice.

We arrived at my dorm, and I was so excited to start a new chapter of my life, even though I didn't end the last chapter. It was a *'to be continued'* placeholder for *unfinished business*. I would soon find that out as my college life began.

I kissed my parents, hurried them out of my dorm, reassuring them that I would be just fine, and watched them drive off. I ran back to my dorm room, jumped up and down on my new bed, and anticipated what my life was going to look like next.

THE EDUCATION

TRAUMA

Trauma is generally a deeply distressing or disturbing experience from what might be considered issues of daily life such as divorce, illness, accidents, violence, rape, and death. Psychological effects include worry and anxiety, while behavioral effects of trauma include sleeping difficulties. According to NCIPC report, trauma is the leading cause of death between the ages of 1 and 46. Medical News Today reported that the annual cost of trauma is $671billion a year in healthcare and in lost productivity.

The severity of traumatic experiences ranges from mild to severe. Mild effects of trauma include insomnia, worry, increased smoking and alcohol. Mild effects of trauma typically don't require medical treatment, so supportive interventions from family and friends can alleviate the symptoms. Moderate effects of trauma include anxiety, rational and irrational fear to which psychological treatment is warranted.

Severe effects of trauma results in psychiatric illnesses like Post Traumatic Stress Disorder, also known as PTSD, as well as Major Depressive Disorder and Schizophrenia. This level of trauma requires specialized treatment for any chance of recovery.

Overall, feelings of helplessness and hopelessness plague traumatized victims, impacting almost every aspect of their life, to which interventions are mandatory for the best hope of recovery and for a normal way of life.

Does any of these resonate with you? Have you experienced any form of trauma? What are your symptoms? What have you done to normalize your way of life?

THE CONVERSATION
LIFE LESSONS

I woke up the next morning in a daze. I was undoubtedly traumatized by what just happened the day before. I felt depressed. I was alone in my dorm room. Alone. "What just happened to me? What did I do wrong to deserve this? He was my friend! I trusted him!" Little did I know that my mind, body, and spirit

SPEAK YOUR VOICE

were formulating a way to protect me from the painful memory of the sexual assault by answering the unanswered question.

WHAT NEXT?

The thoughts I had, called automatic thoughts, resulted in unspoken rules like:

" I have to protect myself at all costs; I'm unlovable, do what is necessary to be loved; I will never trust men; I hate liars; I will NEVER Get Got Again; I will get them before they get me."

These thoughts would serve to protect me and justify my actions yet keep me bound for the next 20 years.

My voice was lost. I searched for it in college.

There is a phrase called *buck wild.* I was buck wild in college. This innocent young virgin before college life, before the sexual assault, goes to college and sleeps with as many guys as she possibly can. Why? To feel loved, to gain friends, to feel important and significant again. Most importantly, to let it be *my choice and decision* to have sex. In full disclosure, I developed a mentality of role reversal. *"I will treat men the way they treat women. I will be the guy, and they will be the girl, and I will put notches on my belt for sure."* Sadly, I internalized my rapist. This is called internalized oppression. In other words, I had begun to mirror the behavior of the one who assaulted me. I was domineering, strong-willed, and quick to shut men down when their ideas, actions, and behaviors didn't line up with what I wanted. I didn't care what they wanted. It was my way or no way at all. I called all the shots, and seemingly, when they found a way out from me, they left. This was my new persona. I was losing myself more and more by the minute.

Yet, I still searched for my voice.

Three years later, I joined a few Christian leadership and Women's groups thanks to great girlfriends like Chelsea and Camilla who supported me during the search for my voice. In fact, I co-developed a Women's group called Ladies of Grace with five other women. It was a group that would meet every Friday to teach first-year students how to respect themselves, how to approach relationships and dating, and how to exercise the buddy system when attending campus parties to prevent date rape. I remember speaking at an event we created on a Saturday, and I candidly shared about my life on campus, choices I had made, and what I had concluded as life lessons in hopes that these young women choose not to do what I did. I received a standing ovation for sharing my story. My voice is starting to whisper.

I obtained a work-study job at the Woman's Center on campus. While on break, I decided to read some books that would help me support the group I was a part of.

I picked a particular one that I was drawn to entitled *Acquaintance Rape*. Surveying it quickly, I said to myself, "Hmm. Looks interesting. Why not? It's short enough. I'll read it." Imagine me sitting with this book covering my face, fervently reading from cover to cover, and ding! A light bulb appears above my head. I dropped the book, and with an astonished look on my face, I spoke my voice:

"Oh, my gosh! I've been raped!"

I didn't know I was raped up to this point. Seriously.

I knew what I experienced wasn't right, but I most certainly did not know it was called acquaintance rape.

I was lost for a long time, and it was now my time to find myself. I called my girlfriend, Cherrea who attended another school of my epiphany. I said, "Oh, my God! Did you know that I just found out that I was raped?!" She laughed and said, "Girl, take a number. We've all been raped at one time or another." My mouth *dropped,* and face astonished again! I said, "What do you mean?" She said, "Do you know the percentage of girls who get raped between the ages of 13 and 24? It's an epidemic, girl, but actually, unfortunately, it's normal. I didn't really know anybody in my circle of friends who had not been raped, except you. Unfortunately, welcome to the club."

My God.

I could not believe this was considered a norm, as a rite of passage for girls to become women or something. *Is this what we have been reduced to? Were we really this insignificant? Were we only to be pleasurable to men, and that's it – nothing more?*

Societal norms seem to suggest that women are inferior to men; the sad part is many women have accepted that. We indeed have lost ourselves. We put on a mask that hides who we are. We pretend to be something we're not. We don't even know how to accept our own selves, and often, we stand around hopelessly waiting for others to accept us. It is our time to search our voices. It is our time to find ourselves.

You may ask, "How? How do I find myself?"

THE REVELATION
TIPS AND RECOMMENDATIONS

Author Alex Elle said, "You're not a victim for sharing your story. You are a survivor setting the world on fire with your truth. And you never know who needs your light, your warmth, and raging courage."

In retrospect, I see what has helped me during my journey of searching my voice while in college. Here are a few tips and recommendations for facing any traumatic experiences or sexual assault, misconduct, or harassment.

- ✓ **Don't isolate** - Normally, after trauma, one may want to withdraw from others, but that only makes things worse, whereas connecting to others face to face will help you heal much more quickly, so make every effort to maintain your relationships and avoid spending too much time alone.
- ✓ **Share your feelings not necessarily the story** - It is crucial to have people you can share your feelings with to prevent from internalizing the trauma, even though you

don't have to relive the trauma by talking about it. Have people who will actively and attentively listen without judgment.

- ✓ **Join a support group.** Spending time with others who have faced similar challenges can help in your recovery Their stories of resilience and hope may inspire you to overcome your trials and tribulations.

- ✓ **Grieving is normal following trauma**: Grief is a natural reaction to loss. Allow yourself to appropriately grieve if you have been assaulted or traumatized. Like people who have lost a loved one, trauma survivors go through a grieving process. It will be easier to cope if you turn to others for support.

- ✓ **Think of your health:** Get enough rest, avoid alcohol and drugs, eat a well-balanced meal, and include positive affirmations to recite in the morning and in the evening for a few minutes before taking to social media and work emails.

- ✓ **Know that it is not the end of the world**. You have your whole life ahead of you. Reach out and make new friends, take a class or join a club to meet people. Reach out to neighbors or colleagues more than ever before.

Let these tips and recommendations prepare you for your journey to finding your voice again.

SELF REFLECTION EXERCISE

To **SEARCH** Your Voice, get into a quiet space, and give yourself 15-30 minutes to do this exercise. Reflect, free associate, and write down your first thoughts that come to mind when answering the questions below without questioning or altering your answers.

Write down what you remember as far as your standards and values. What are the principles you stand for and why?

_____
_____
_____

Share your experience. What has happened in your life that you aren't proud of? What were notable thoughts and feelings that resulted from your experience? What were your behavior patterns?

_____
_____
_____

Life Lessons Learned: What did you learn that you can share with others who may go through similar ordeals?

_____
_____
_____

What new professional or personal group do you commit to joining in support of searching your voice?

_____
_____
_____

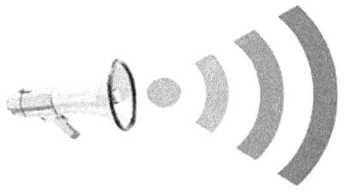

INTERLUDE #1
SARAH, ME TOO

Hi Sarah! Thank you for sharing your story! I have wanted to "speak my voice for years now. I have never spoken out... and I'm still hesitant to do so... more for fear of hurting my parents. I was molested for many years from the time I was around 4. I didn't get help for it until 2013 AFTER I had my 4th child. So much I still work through on a daily basis. But I have a desire to use what happened to me to help others. Sexual abuse is so prevalent in my culture and thus not addressed. My mom still refuses to believe me, and my dad still has no clue. I believe God is using you somehow to push me along in this.

So here it goes....

My earliest memories of my childhood consist of some pleasant thoughts, including times spent traveling with my parents and brother, hosting dinners every month for my huge family and my parents helping many families come over from their homeland and settle into a new country. I feel proud of my background/culture where helping my family and supporting one another is a major part of who we are. But if I stay in the moment too long, my mind goes to a place of some not so good memories. Ones of feeling alone, ashamed, disgusted, embarrassed and hurt. These feelings were caused by a few of these very same family members who make up my large family that I am "proud of." Confusing, huh? That is pretty much how I have lived my entire life. Confused. How could I feel so proud of this wonderful big family of mine when within this family were people that hurt me and affected the way I lived most of my 40 years of life? It has not been an easy road. Almost 40 years later, I still deal with feelings, emotions, and thoughts that remind me of the dark memories I dealt with as a child. My first dark memory is one of me sitting in the bathtub at the young of 4 feeling very embarrassed and ashamed as one of my male relatives sat next to the tub, smoking his cigarette watching me bathe. I felt frozen. I scrunched up in the tub trying not to let him see my private parts. I feel like I was crying out but no one could hear me. Several other similar memories pop up here, and there was when I was in the presence of a male relative who was looking and even in later incidents, was touching and holding me in ways that were inappropriate and felt very wrong to me. I had tried to cry out to a family member who dismissed me and didn't believe anything I had to say. These incidents of sexual molestation and abuse occurred until I was in high school. They stopped only when I mustered up the guts to tell one of my male relatives that if he ever touched me again, I would go straight to the police. The next weekend I left for college, 4 hours away from home. From then on, every decision I made was one from a place of hurt, trauma, low self-esteem and worthlessness. I made mistakes left and right but somehow felt justified in making them. For years, I suppressed these dark childhood memories up until I experienced the most stressful time in my life. I was experiencing some postpartum depression that left me with PTSD. I was at a point in my life where I could not go on unless I dealt with this very real part of my life. This is the moment I had to face all that "darkness" that I had experienced. Through many prayers, the support of my husband, a spiritual counselor and a psychologist, I began my journey to healing. Four years later, I am a new person. I am not a victim but a victor of my life. I realize what I went through has a bigger purpose, and I am ready to step into that purpose. Those feelings of hurt, shame, and embarrassment are long gone. I know what happened to me is not a result of who I was but a result of the insecurities and weakness of the men that were responsible for it. I am grateful for my life and am empowered to Speak My Voice and help others become victors as well.

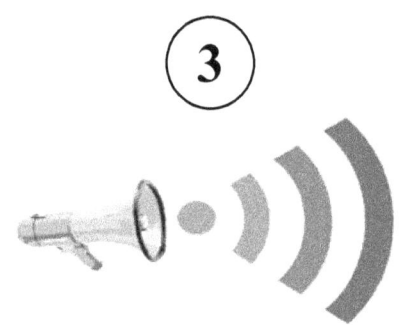

FIND YOUR VOICE

WHERE YOU LOSE IT

Sometimes when you lose your way, you find YOURSELF"

– MANDY HALE.

SPEAK YOUR VOICE
MY NARRATIVE

I ended my work-study program with the Women's Center as I approached graduation. I was excited that my three- year college experience was coming to a close, yet, I was stumped with not knowing my next steps: "Should I go on for my master's degree in Psychology? What school should I pursue?" Lord knows I had some defining moments during my college years. Good and not so good choices I had made, friends and enemies I have developed, and *"Oh, Sarah, so you have been raped. Get over it and join the club. You aren't the first and definitely not the last"*—an unforgettable remark shared by my girlfriend after I told her of my *ah-ha moment* in the Women's Center after reading about Acquaintance Rape.

Yes, fun times at college.

Oh, by the way, I did not do the five-year plan like other college students. I had too much pride to be behind fellow high school classmates who started college a year before me. I decided to go through all semesters non stop, including summers, to graduate with them in 1998. I was always hard working, an ambitious go-getter all of my life, but in these three years at the university, I was exceptionally hardworking. I worked harder because I masked the sexual assault that robbed me and left me for dead just moments before entering college for the first time. Even though I worked hard, I graduated with a 2.67 GPA. I was devastated. I was nearly a straight A student throughout my formative years, and to get a 2.67 really hurt. Looking back now as a Licensed Professional Counselor, I know that being raped played a significant impact on my life.

Often, the effects of violations experienced can show up in your behavior, attitude, thinking, patterns, and habits. To help deal or avoid the pain, we develop defense mechanisms. My defense mechanism was to *detach*. I detached from reality and from my own self. I felt fractured, bankrupted, and disconnected because I had experienced a traumatic event that did not connect with my values, standards or philosophies. And now, I was preparing to return home and risk seeing him again. *It was time to find my voice.*

Now back home, I started looking for him on the block. I did not go to his home. I couldn't. I waited until I saw him at the corner store. Questions ran through my mind like, *"Was I going to be the one to break the ice, to take the high road to be friends again, to put the incident behind us?"*

By this point, I had a new identity. I was a college grad, but didn't feel anything special about myself. My virginity was my secret sauce, my superpower. It made me stand out. I put so much pride into being a virgin because I felt different and unique. To give context, the expectation of young *black* girls in my neighborhood was low. We were predicted to fall into the "ghettoized" system, which meant living on welfare, having 3 or 4 kids by different baby daddies, staying with our parents, and so on.

I defied the odds and the stereotypes and had much to be proud of. Yet, I still felt insignificant and flat-out worthless upon returning home from college.

I saw him at the corner store of 24th and Somerset, and instantly the wound reopened. I needed answers from him. I supposed deep inside I wanted to bury it all and pretend like the rape never happened and to just move on and forgive as it is the Christian way. I demonstrated a sense of excitement to see him after all these years. When he saw me, he shocked me. He acted as if I wasn't even there. I asked, *"What's going on? I thought we were friends."*

He treated me like I was some sort of groupie – *'sweating him'* – looking for some attention and affection. And guess what? That's *exactly* how the scene played out. I was literally sweating him, begging for him to take notice and talk to me. I wanted him to hear my voice, but I lost my voice. Again. He muted my voice.

I was perplexed that he was deliberately not speaking to me and choosing not to take notice of my presence. This added a new narrative that I had about females. He reinforced my automatic thought that I was insignificant, nothing, worthless, and only good for one thing. It also supplemented my attitude to treat men like they treat women. I couldn't believe how I was being treated, how all of this was going down. *"Is this really the life and world I was born into? How did it all come to this?"* I believe the beginning point of losing my voice happened way before I was raped.

When I was thirteen, I was in an abusive relationship. You may ask, how in the world can a thirteen-year-old girl be in an abusive relationship? Easily, by having a boyfriend who gives you black eyes, chases you with his German Shepherds to bite you, or has a bunch of boys *jump you*– beating, punching, kicking and holding you to throw urine in your face. Can you believe that? He peed in a cup and threw urine on my face.

While I exercised forgiveness and turned the other cheek and sympathized to what others were going through as a result of their perpetrators' behaviors, I thought it unfair that we the victims are held accountable for their decisions and behavior. Consequentially, I learned a trick or two as a result on how to employ the 3 Ds of Defense Mechanisms-- *to disappear, disengage, and disconnect* to protect myself. Have you ever engaged in the 3D formula before?

This is where my thoughts about guys came to a head. When I told my brothers – because I couldn't hide the last black eye I had one of them questioned me about it, and then said he *was not going to defend me*. Flustered by that, I asked him, "Why not?" He told me, *"Because you're going to go right back to him. That's what females do. They'll get beat up and beat down, but they always go back to the boy."*

When I was beaten by my boyfriend and his friends that fateful summer night in 1990, I remembered what my brothers said, *"We are not going to defend you. You will just go back to the boy."* I reframed my mindset about my brothers. I fed myself a false narrative, or story, that my brothers *would* protect me, and if I told all 5 of my brothers, they would kill every boy that harmed me and go to jail as a result. This tactic was to keep my relationship and respect for my brothers intact because otherwise, it created more unspoken rules for my protection--- *"I have to protect myself at all costs because I cannot depend on men to protect me. Men act weak like women sometimes, so I have to act like the man to defend myself from others, and apparently from them, too."*

Where is my voice? I lost it. Can you help me find it?

THE EDUCATION

STOCKHOLM SYNDROME

Stockholm syndrome is classified as a condition that causes a psychological coalition between the captive and the captors. The term Stockholm Syndrome was created by criminologist and psychiatrist Nils Bejerot. He explained how in 1973 four bank workers were held captive by bank robbers and how the hostages developed some form of positive relationship with the robbers' six-day standoff. Psychologist Dr. Frank Ochberg further explained what it is. Victims experience a terrifying event to which their perpetrator provides some form of comfort that triggers gratitude and positive regard by the victims for the perpetrator, without thinking that the perpetrator is the one that put them in the terrifying situation to begin with.

Demonstrations of Stockholm Syndrome are forms of abuse, such as the partner having a sense of dependency on their intimate partner and stays with the perpetrator even through the abuse, or the child who is physically or emotionally abused and yet the child is protective towards their parent. There is a famous case of a woman who had stolen a child at birth from a hospital and raised the child for 18 years. The story made national headlines when the truth came out that the woman had kidnapped the young girl at birth and was arrested. The young girl who was abducted showed loyalty and refuse to testify against the woman she has known as Mom for 18 years. The young girl reunited with her biological parents and started calling her the name they had first given her at birth, but the young girl responds to the name the kidnapper named her.

Regarding sexual assault, victims can become protective and loyal to their perpetrators, and lie or avoid discussing the assault, harassment, or misconduct.

Do you or someone you know ever experienced Stockholm syndrome? It is ok to admit if you pledged loyalty towards the perpetrator. This book will help you break free from that mentality by way of awareness and the tools necessary to stay free and Speak Your Voice.

THE CONVERSATION

LIFE LESSONS

My parents were born in the 40s and raised in North Carolina in the 50s before moving to Philadelphia in the 60s where they met and began their new lives together. Momma was quiet, meek and shy. She spoke her voice only when she had something to say. My dad was more outgoing and very talkative and the head of the household. I was watching my parents' entire interaction and exchanges with one another. From my understanding, Southern Black men adopted the philosophy that women were *to be seen and not heard*. Although my dad never mistreated my mom, he was emotionally unavailable, thinking that *showing up and being there for the family* was good enough. In his mind, remaining at home and taking care of his responsibilities, keeping a job, and paying the bills were all demonstrations of love for us. But that was it. He didn't give anything else. My parents' interactions and lack thereof began adding to my automatic thoughts.

"*Men are disrespectful. Men do not show real love. Women only speak their voices when they have someone compelling to say and then shut up afterward. Men are not emotionally available at all.*"

My dad displayed some pretty chauvinistic ways toward my mom. I remember my mom called him on it one day and my dad was so angry, I never saw him that mad.

Truth hurts.

I developed these newfound truths about males at 13 years old. My *'once upon a time knight in shining armor'* view of males, and females as *'damsels in distress,'* quickly turned into *males vs. females, superior vs. inferior, dominant vs. subordinate* perspectives, reinforced by my dad and brothers and my abusive boyfriend and his crew.

I now believed that *female voices do not matter.*

WARNING: The Story Gets Worse. When I returned home from college, many of my male friends were giving me the cold shoulder. I didn't know if it was my assumption or if I was correct in my assumption. I met up with a really good friend of mine named Shomari. He has given me the cold shoulder! *"What did I do wrong now?"*

He did not open up at first, but after pressing him for answers, he finally shared why the guys from around our way were acting so mean to me. Things were awkward. There were so many pieces missing from the whole equation that seemed to take a life of its own.

Those who I grew up with call me by my middle name, Renee. Throughout my formative years from kindergarten to 12th grade, I was called by my first name, Sarah. Please place a mental bookmarker on this poignant point about my first and middle names. I will share more about it towards the end of the chapter.

"Renee, I am very mad at the fact that you are no different than any of the girls around here. I was rooting for you. I thought you were different."

"I am different, but what are you talking about?"

"I'm talking about you and him."

"What about me and him?"

"He's been going around bragging about how he was able to sleep with you."

SPEAK YOUR VOICE

Now here is the moment that broke everything and changed my life forever. I have frozen in time once again. The first time was with the rape. The second time was with my abusive boyfriend. The third time was with my brothers telling me they won't protect me because I will go back to my abusive boyfriend. Now, here I am, having to make a choice, to make a decision. Either I speak my voice and tell Shomari what happened that fateful day, or keep my voice on mute and not tell him anything and continue suffering in silence. I had enough ego strength that I built up during college, to speak my voice.

"Wait a minute! HE RAPED ME!"

Everything froze again. What Shomari would say next could change everything. It could go either way. Either way would be monumental.

My expectation for Shomari was to side with me and say, *"You know what? I'm going to beat him down and serve you some justice."* I sincerely hoped Shomari would believe me. Besides Cherrea, Shomari was the second friend I told about being sexually assaulted. I knew I couldn't tell my five brothers because if I told them this guy raped me, they were going to jail for murder. *That's the lie I told myself.* I didn't believe my brothers would do anything because they said they wouldn't help me when I was getting beat up by my boyfriend. Why would they do something about me being raped? I pretended like they were going *to be real men* fighting and dying for my honor by protecting their little sister and serving her justice. But, what are real men? I certainly was confused by my own philosophy without having an actual prototype to compare what a real man was.

Shomari responded to my answer and said this:

"I don't believe you."

Can you imagine the blood rushing from my body to the floor? Here was yet another guy that I trusted, that I opened up to, to tell him what had happened to me, and he didn't even believe me.

"Why in the world would you not believe me? Why do you think I would make that shit up?" I said.

"This is what really happened, Renee. We were talking about you one night, and we said, 'You know, what if you wanted to get with any girl from around here, who would it be?' We named some names and then when we called your name out, everybody said, 'Oh no! Not Renee! Nobody can touch Renee. She's a virgin, she's a goodie two shoes, she out of our league, she's a Christian. She doesn't want to give it up. And dude said, 'You know what, I can do it. I bet I can get some. I can sleep with her.' We said, 'No way, man. Get out of here! No, you can't. You can't touch her. She won't give it up.' He said, 'You wanna bet?' We were like, 'Yeah. How much?' And he said, 'I bet you $30 I can sleep with Renee.' We said, 'Okay, it's on.' We put up the money and off he went. He came back and told us, 'Hey, guess what? I got it!' We were falling all over each other saying, 'Get out of here, man! No, you didn't.' He was like, 'Yes I did!'"

And without verifying this information, they paid him. $30.

I *was worth* $30!

That sealed it for me. Any strength, self-worth, self-confidence, any hope for humanity, any piece of voice that I found and started piecing together, all disintegrated at that very moment.

I lost my voice. So I created a new one. One that was filled with hatred, malicious and revenge. Opinionated, tell it like it is, strong-willed Renee was going to show them all, while quiet, meek, innocent Sarah takes a back seat for Renee to protect Sarah's decency and honor. This is Dissociation at its finest. Renee was the knight in shining armor and Sarah was the damsel in distress. This was my way of protecting myself. It's cool to be both hood and classy. Versatile! No, it's my cry for help.

THE REVELATION
TIPS AND RECOMMENDATIONS

As I share my stories with you, understand that it is not always easy to bring up the past, but facing it to move forward is entirely worth it. I had to do it. So while I may introduce you to new norms and new philosophies and new ways of thinking, keep in mind that at one point, my thoughts were very skewed. I was born a female acting like a male to be accepted in my family, to protect myself from other males because I didn't trust them, and I didn't like how females were viewed or treated. Society has done a pretty good job at justifying my argument, yet and still, I realized I had built these fortresses around my heart. Here's the thing, the fortress protects against what comes in, but locks up what's already in.

How can anyone find their voice locked up?

Powerful person, here are some thoughts to ponder:

- ✓ Where did you lose your voice? This is a critical question because where you think you lost your voice may not actually be where you lost it. It probably goes back further than you realize.

- ✓ Go back in time and start from the beginning. You need to go back in time and search yourself to find your voice. Making the decision to peel back the layers of your past, even going back a generation or two will be to your advantage as you seek to speak your voice.

- ✓ Know that you have a choice to find your voice, or not find your voice. Business and Life Coach guru, the late Jim Rohn, talked about how it is easy to change, just as it is easy not to change. Nothing will change around us unless we change ourselves first. You have a choice to find your voice for your own peace of mind. And you have the choice not to find your voice and remain the same.

- ✓ Don't complain about your current state of affairs if you aren't doing anything to change it. Additionally, do not dwell in the realm of indecisiveness and stay stuck. Make a move and make a choice.

SPEAK YOUR VOICE

✓ It is not about what you lost anyway. It is about the opportunities you gain to ultimately speak your voice. It should be a priority to find your voice. There are others in need of your voice. I encourage you to find it.

Think it through as you find your voice. It takes guts to go back to the beginning of where it all happened to find it, but this time better than ever.

Just remember the golden rule.

Seek, and you shall find.

SELF REFLECTION EXERCISE

To **FIND** Your Voice, get into a quiet space, and give yourself 15-30 minutes to do this exercise. Reflect, free associate, and write down your first thoughts that come to mind when answering the questions below without questioning or altering your answers.

What are your best qualities that people praise you for? Write them here:

_____
_____
_____

What are your intentions when it comes to speaking your voice? What do you want to say? What do you want the world to know?

_____
_____
_____

What type of lifestyle do you want to have as a result of finding your voice? What type of lifestyle do you see in your heart that you want to make a reality?

_____
_____
_____

Embrace Your Emotions: Note the feelings that comes up while you do this exercise here:

_____
_____
_____

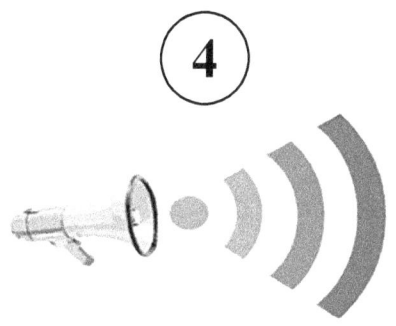

GET YOUR VOICE

GET YOUR OWN IDENTITY

"You cannot make yourself have a flashback, nor will you have one unless you are emotionally ready to remember something. Once remembered, the memory can help you to face more of the truth. You can then express your pent-up feelings about the memory and continue on your path to recovery."

— Beverly Engel, *The Right to Innocence*

Sarah Renee Langley

MY NARRATIVE

HE RAPED ME! I exclaimed with such power, confident that my friend Shomari would believe me. I didn't choose to give anything up. That guy not only took my virginity---my identity, but my power, my confidence, my life, my voice. Shomari didn't believe me, and I didn't understand why. He couldn't tell me why. Now I had to figure out how to clear my name and get my identity back. I had to figure out how to get my voice back.

I went looking for him again. I went right to his house. Amazing. I was angry. Felt totally mistreated. Flashback. I remember when someone jumped my brother Jon for his hat. I called my girl Nadira and said, "We have business to take care of."

"We are going to Meady's house right now." I was enraged. I did not think or blink as to what would happen to me. After all, I am preparing to fight a guy over my brother's honor. Something they were supposed to do for my honor.

We went to Meady's house, and his little cousin answered the door. "Hey, are you the freaks my cousin is waiting for?" I said, "Um, yeah, we're the freaks," as I looked at Nadira to play it cool. "Oh, well he's not here." Nadira and I left until the little boy called us from down the street. He said, "Hey freaks! Here goes my cousin." Meady looking at us perplexed, recognizing we were the wrong freaks. I said, "I don't want any trouble, just my brother's hat." He said, "Man, I don't have his hat get the fuck outta here." "I said I'm not going anywhere until I get my brother's hat back!"

"Yall better get outta here!" And he walks away. As soon as we reached the end of the block, Nadira screamed, "LOOK OUT!" The boy had a broken beer bottle and was about to use it on me. I scared him and myself the more. "Please use it on me! Give me a reason to fuck you up right now! Please do it!" Looking more fearful than ever, he throws the bottle down and says, "Y'all better get the fuck from around here."

As Nadira and I walked home, that rage dissipated and fear overtook me. I could not believe what happened. I totally saw black and red when my brother Jon told me this guy took his hat.

That same rage was upon me now as I knocked on his door to protect my honor.

He opens the door, and I come in. I confront him on this entire bet and that what happened was not consensual. *"I don't know what you are talking about!"*

"Nigga, you raped me! I didn't give it up to you!"

"Go ahead with all of that Renee!" Flashback. I was in my 6th-grade homeroom class, and Johnny came to my desk once again to pick on me. His friend Maurice started to pull him away from me and begged him to just leave me alone. The kids were laughing, Johnny still picking with me, calling me names, and I sat there stewing. I have reached my tolerance threshold of being picked on at that point. I decided to take matters into my own hands. This quiet storm (me) took one of those thick-ass geometry textbooks, and with all my might, smacked Johnny clear across his face, as he went straight down the aisle .

The OOOHHHs and laughter filled the classroom air.

Apparently, this is typical behavior when I am pushed to my limits.

Likewise, I grabbed the very long, thick, double play VCR box and threw it right at my rapist, hitting his knees.

Time froze.

I snapped out of my rage and became fearful again. I realized where I was and who was in front of me. He looked at me in pure anger. I was afraid. He didn't move. I backed out of the living room of his house opened the door and walked out. I ran home, ran upstairs to my room and began to cry.

I did not know who I was and what I was experiencing. Most importantly, I did not understand why.

Powerful people ask powerful questions. Powerful person, *"Who are you? Do you know who you are? Do you know what difference you make? Do you know what you carry?"*

I'm not talking about a gun, knife, or any kind of weapon that you carry. But I would understand if you did nowadays. I'm simply asking if you know who you are and what you possess within.

SPEAK YOUR VOICE

I decided I could not live in North Philly again. I outgrew my neighborhood since being away in college. I needed to escape again. I decided to continue with my academic career, especially since my best friend, Melissa was in her doctoral program and I wanted to catch up with her. Obtaining my doctorate was always in view. I figured that was the ultimate academic completion, so why not go all the way and finish my schooling.

I started my master's program after working in the mental health field for three years. I remember when I was in the 11th grade in high school, I asked my friend, Cherrea, "Hey, what do you want to be when you grow up?"

"I'm going to be a psychologist."

"You know what? I'm going to be a psychologist, too because you're my friend, and if you're going to be a psychologist, I'm going to be a psychologist, too!"

This same friend changed her mind and decided to be a chemist because her boyfriend at the time was going into chemistry, I think. Oh, well. Even then I decided to stick with psychology and decided to become a counselor.

Quick story. I wanted to be a fashion designer, singer, novelist, and lawyer. My brothers talked me out of just about every single one! "There's no money in fashion design… you can't sing…. you can't write, and there's no money in that anyway…if you take a case and you lose it for your client, they will come back and kill you!"

Can't make this up. Don't hate my brothers. I don't.

I said to myself, "The next profession I pick I am sticking to it no matter what!" I told them I am going to be a counselor. "Don't do that! If you get a crazy person, they will kill you, and you will die!"

"I DON'T CARE!" I clapped back at them. "I am sticking with this psychology thing, and that's it!"

And I did for the next 20 years.

In retrospect, I know that going into psychology was predestined. While my initial decision to enter into psychology started with my girlfriend's decision, it would be two years later that I would be raped, go to college to become a clinical psychotherapist, and help other rape victims to get their power back, and even write about it. Therefore, I say, do not curse small beginnings no matter how small and how they start. All things do work together for your good and for the good of others in the end. Besides, the other professions my brothers talked me out of never left me.

I published a few books, have been part of singing groups, have a keen eye for fashion (thanks to my Model Mom), and I certainly know how to gather evidence and argue my points to the T!

What is meant for you to become is meant for you to become

I love mentors! My dad has been full of wisdom and shared his wise instructions with my brothers and me every Sunday after church. I also come from a family of wise old souls. I love gleaning and getting information that helps me to grow wherever I can.

Having a mentor was another way to get my voice. When I was in college, I had this great mentor who worked in the financial aid office name Mrs. Patterson. She always provided wisdom and knowledge and became like a second mom and low-key therapist for me. I just loved her; petite and beautiful, so strong-willed and boisterous. Mrs. Patterson was always in the forefront as an elegant, accomplished and competent Black Woman, gaining the respect of prominent professionals at the university. Behind the scenes, she was a *sistahgirl*, vocal, to the point, quite a matter of fact. I admired her versatility and how she *spoke her voice*. Mrs. Patterson knew how to play the professional game. When people assumed they were ahead of her, she was really ahead of them. I wanted to be just like Mrs. Patterson when I grew up.

She also reminded me of my mom because mom was the one running everything behind the scenes, while systematically and strategically making my dad shine as the head of the household. Mom was brilliant at making others look great as she receded into the background. My mom made the saying, *'Behind every good man is a very good woman'* as truth. My question is, why is it that the woman has to be behind the man for him to be good? Why not be beside him or ahead of him? That is another chapter for another book.

I was blessed to have such great mentors to help me get my

voice and my identity. I searched to mirror a healthy identity who knew how to speak their voice. Unfortunately, my fear was mirroring and becoming others' identities as opposed to becoming who I was designed to become. While I had Mrs. Patterson and my Mom as perfect examples, I didn't fully appreciate what I had in them, and I searched elsewhere. Sometimes I searched in the wrong places for that identity and voice to pattern after based on popularity and societal standards.

Powerful person, let me ask you some powerful questions. *Have you ever thought how often you compared yourself to other people? Have you thought about how society sets this standard for how women are to be the most beautiful, the most ambitious, or the most phenomenal of all? Are you waiting for validation and looking for permission from a society that is full of its own drama and fakeness? validation and looking for permission from a society that is full of its own drama and fakeness?*

Simply put, *what's up with your own voice?*

THE EDUCATION

STAGES OF PSYCHOSOCIAL DEVELOPMENT

Erikson's stages of psychosocial development stem from the psychoanalytic theory that identifies healthy human development and growth from infancy to adulthood. According to developmental psychologist Erik Erickson, successful completion of his Stages of Psychosocial Development results in a healthy ego strength and fundamental tools to deal with crises and proceed to your next level of self-actualization. This means you will pass the grade if you have developed a mature character to get to the next level of character growth. Consequently, failure to successfully complete a stage results in an unhealthy personality ego and sense of self. This simply means you will be stuck from graduating to the next level until you build your character at the level you are to proceed to.

Ages 18 to 35 exclaim, *"Who am I? Who do I connect with?"* Ages 35-40 ask the questions, *"What's my purpose? How do I leave a mark in the world?"* Ages 40-45 pose the thoughts, *"I'm not missing out! It's my turn now!"* Ages 45-50 declare, *What's Next? What to Do Now?"*

Does any of these sound familiar?

I have combined some stages by age to discuss my points. Erickson's psychosocial stage for ages 18-40 is called Intimacy versus Isolation. In this stage, one will share themselves more intimately and explore long-term relationships. Completing this stage successfully results in the sense of commitment and safety in relationships. However, failure to successfully complete this stage results in avoidance, isolation, loneliness, and depression.

Erickson's psychosocial stage for ages 40-65 is called Generativity versus Stagnation. In this stage, one will establish their careers, raise children, and become involved in community organizations and activities. One would feel very productive and feel accomplished in their endeavors and desire to give back. However, failure to complete this stage successfully results in stagnation and feeling unproductive.

It is important to note that mastering each stage to get to the next is not required. Instead, it is based on what you have learned, and which polarized force you gravitate to that determines if you pass and proceed or fail and remain until you gain enough and gather enough ego strength to deal with the next level.

There is a saying, 'New levels, new devils.' To deal with the next level of devils, you have to first conquer the last devils. To get your voice and identity, you have to know the stage of life you are in and make it a point to learn, grow, and develop your character to proceed until you finally reach your destination of greatness and help others achieve theirs as well.

What stage are you in to get your voice? How is it going? Are you mastering or failing your stage? What do you need to do differently to proceed to the next level?

THE CONVERSATION

LIFE LESSONS

In my book, I*t's Your Turn Now! 7 Secrets To Living Life on Your Own Terms,* I discuss the three masks that we all tend to wear. The first one is the perfect mask, the second is the performer mask, and the third is the dark mask. If you wish to order the full version of my book, please go to my website, drsarahreneelangley.com for purchase. If you want the free mini digital download, you can go to my website and grab your copyt today.

I love makeup. I love the way it enhances my beauty. NOTE: Makeup enhances, not beautifies. Beauty comes from within and shines out. The *perfect mask* is what we put on to cover up ourselves, and we pretend to be who we want to be, making adjustments every now and then till we transform into an identity we think people want to see.

The *performer mask* surfaces when people start to see through the perfect mask. They notice the blemishes, the dark circles, the nose that isn't constructed right, and the chin that doesn't have the dimple in the right spot. When *'they' (have you ever asked who 'they' are?)* start to question our perfect mask, we defend and avoid interrogation from people who really want to know what is behind our mask.

The *dark mask* is the one I didn't want anybody, even myself, ever to see. This mask covers up what you internalized as real about yourself. This dark mask covers insignificance, worthlessness, feelings of nothingness.

Do you identify with any of these masks? My identity was made up of all three. It is unfortunate we have to undergo that very exhausting task of putting on the mask we think is acceptable to others, not realizing it destroys any hope of getting our voices and discovering who we really are. Putting on the mask prevents us from being authentic and inevitably becoming who we were already designed to be.

Think about it, how can we get our voices if we don't have an identity to assign the voice to?

THE REVELATION

TIPS AND RECOMMENDATIONS

While it is normal to struggle with our identity in our early years, wanting to be like everyone else is hard to manage because you were designed to be different. Fake identities will be found and lost several times until we take time to get our own authentic voice and build our real identity around it.

Circumstances may make it difficult to identify your voice, but make up in your mind to throw away those masks, un-follow the script, break the norm and take back the ownership and accountability of your dear life. Only then will your real identity *grow forth.*

Remember, no one can be like you other than you, so be you because everyone else is taken. To further supplemental this point on how to get your voice, do the following:

- ✓ Do not spend your entire life at the mercy of your past. Think of the past as depression. It is in the past. You cannot change it, so why get depressed over something you cannot change?
- ✓ Do not spend your entire time majoring on minor things. Jim Rohn shared how not to major in the minor. Don't put thought or time into the future. Actually, think of your future as anxiety. You are getting anxious about

things that have yet to happen.

- ✓ Do not be held down by the opinions of others. We all have filters based on our own values, beliefs, and philosophies. Go to the beat of your own drum and start setting or establishing boundaries and standards to follow for successfully getting your voice.
- ✓ Let go of limiting beliefs. Stop looking at what's missing in your life, or what you don't have, or failures you have had that do not serve anyone. Look at what you do have. Look at what you do possess. No longer lament over what is lost or taken. Instead, renew your shine, reclaim your time, and reinvent your life. *How, you ask?*
- ✓ Renew your shine, reclaim your time, and reinvent your life by saying this word, SATORI. Satori is a Japanese Buddhist term for *'awakening, comprehension, understanding, enlightenment.'*

The enlightenment is this: Stay in the Present Moment. When Depression (your past) and the Anxiety (your future) comes to get your voice and rob you of your identity, say *SATORI*, to reset and refocus on the here and now. It is when you are in the present moment that you come to realize it is a journey and a process to learn and to grow to actualize and to share with others for their growth. That's it. This is the epitome of life.

When you accept these terms and reframe the reasons why you went through what you have as merely life lessons, that is when you will get your voice and become your true authentic self.

SATORI.

Sarah Renee Langley

SELF REFLECTION EXERCISE

To **GET** Your Voice, get into a quiet space, and give yourself 15-30 minutes to do this exercise. Reflect, free associate, and write down your first thoughts that come to mind when answering the questions below without questioning or altering your answers.

What is your Why? What do you think is the reason for your existence?

_____
_____
_____

Look back at the injustices witnessed and experienced. Imagine your passion and your anger surrounding the circumstances. If you were in position to change that injustice, what is it and how would you change it?

_____
_____
_____

What have been your limiting beliefs about yourself, others, and the world? What beliefs are you willing to change?

_____
_____
_____

What mask did you find yourself wearing the most and why? What are you willing to commit to take the mask off?

_____
_____
_____

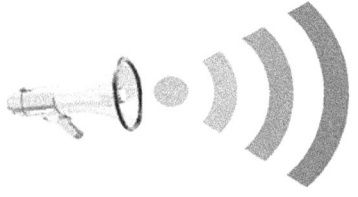

INTERLUDE #2

SARAH, ME TOO

The earliest memory I have of being fondled, or molested, occurred when I would stay with my grandparents. During summer vacations and major holidays every year for as long as I can remember growing up, I would spend the entire summer with my grandparents.

Anyway, I am six years older than my brother, and my uncle, who is the baby of six children, my mom's baby brother, was seven years older than me. So again, as long as I have known myself, he's been there. I considered him as an older brother as opposed to being my uncle. I didn't call him Uncle so-and-so, as I do now, because we acted like brother and sister, and my mother used to say that he'd cry like a baby when it was time for me to leave at the end of every summer or holiday. He'd always been my playmate. We grew up together.

As I began to get older and to develop, that's when things started to shift. When I would sit or lay on the couch watching television, and grandma was apparently not around...she'd be in the kitchen or out in the backyard or up the street talking with neighbors, and I would be alone with my cousin/big brother. I remember him sitting on the floor right next to me, and he would take his hand and fumble to get to my vagina area, and he would finger me. He would somehow get into my panties and finger me. For the life of me, I can't remember what my reaction was the first time he attempted it. I may have recoiled and kicked him or something, but I know that by the second time and every time after that, I would open my legs to him and let him explore my private area. I didn't know the names given to my private area back then like "coochie" or "pussy" yet (I'd learn that terminology in Junior High), but during those few years, when I was seven and eight years old, in the bathtub or in the bed, I would take my own finger and go down there to explore myself to see what the big deal was for him. I didn't know what I was supposed to feel, just like I didn't feel anything necessarily when he did it, but there was some fascination with the whole notion that I had allowed him into my private area and that he had introduced me to a part of myself that I never knew really existed other than it being associated with going to the bathroom. At that age, I didn't even have my menstrual cycle yet, so there was no other function or for that part of my body.

Again, I am not sure how I felt about it or even how to classify our relationship. Maybe this was normal for all siblings, or how big brothers treated little sisters, I didn't know.

    I suppose that I considered it a secret that we had or shared, or if he just considered me his little personal plaything. We were playmates, after all. He never told me not to say anything to anybody, but because that was a private area, I thought that it was a secret and that it should be private. I wasn't supposed to tell, so I didn't. Maybe he wished that I would be his girlfriend, but that couldn't be because we were kin. I know that I was always subconsciously jealous of any girl that would come around the house talking to him and carrying on (because they too were 7 years older and were teenagers like him and I was just the little girl). But because of the secret activity we shared, I guess in my mind I knew I had the upper hand somehow and was "special" to him in a way that the other girls wish they had, or at least that's how I thought about it in my young adolescent mind. So I never said anything. I do remember being angry a lot though when it came to him.

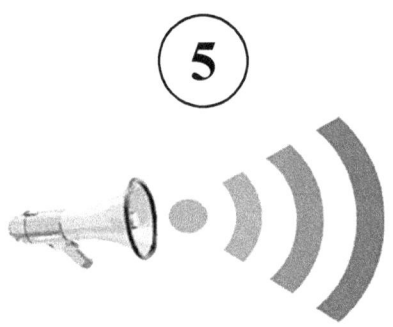

BUILD YOUR VOICE

START FROM THE BEGINNING

"A difficult time can be more readily endured if we retain the conviction that our existence holds a purpose, a cause to pursue, a person to love, a goal to achieve."

– *John Maxwell*

SPEAK YOUR VOICE

MY NARRATIVE

It's timeto take off the masks, burn them so that we no longer have access to them, and embrace our true authentic selves. We realize that those crummy masks don't serve anyone but keep the *stinkin' thinkin'* going. It is like putting a band-aid on an old wound that awaits to be healed. It is time to look at and do everything differently to get different results. Declare this day as a new day to build your voice and start from the beginning. In the Holy Bible, Lamentations 3:23 proclaims, *"Great is his faithfulness; his mercies begin afresh each morning"* (NIV). To me, that means we are given a clean slate. We're given a brush and a blank canvas on which to paint the picture we want to have. We visualize from our own mind and from our own heart which we are to become which holds the key to building our voices.

I shared my reasons for going into the mental health field. It had allowed me counsel a broader audience, especially women who had similar experiences like I had. I wanted to play a small part in setting the captives free by showing them step by step how to build the necessary tools from their life lessons to make choices to be and stay free. I envisioned my clients doing their own thing and living life on purpose. That required for me to build my own voice by being self-employed to employ my unique style of clinical counseling. It also helped me to let go of the sexual assault narrative and move on to turn that obstacle into an opportunity to help others get free.

During my master's internship program, I met Linda, my clinical supervisor. She was leaving my community clinic to pursue her own clinical practice.

Linda helped me through my entrepreneurial journey—one that I never thought I would take because I didn't see myself as my own boss, and she helped coach me in preparation of my private clinical practice. One time, I did not respect her time by showing up late and canceling on her hours within our appointment time. Linda changed all that by having me invest in her services at the full price and charge me if I was a minute late for our clinical supervision. I was never late and never canceled again! Linda helped me build my character, and she helped position me to garner my first client right away. *Never curse what seems to be a curse.* It may be a blessing in disguise to further build your character and your voice.

One time, I had to sit out an entire year when my professor failed me in my first practicum. I was absolutely unequivocally devastated, and life to me was over. I laid on my bed looking up at the ceiling in shock for a day and a half because my professor thought I wasn't ready to move forward with my internship. She messed my plans up! I wanted to graduate in two years. Now it will be three years. There was nothing that I could do but in the meantime, learn some more. I had taken additional courses throughout the year until internship came around again.

One year later, the state of Pennsylvania passed guidelines that allowed master level students to obtain their licenses, provided they met state requirements. One of the conditions was you had to have 60-course credits to apply. Had not my professor failed me, I would have graduated with 48 credits. That meant I would not have been eligible for licensure and would have had to return to school to pick up 12 more credits.

Get it? Don't curse what could be a blessing in disguise.

I passed my repeat practicum with flying colors and began the process of building clinical hours to take the state exam for my professional counselor license.

I was one step closer to building my voice.

To double and triple my efforts in obtaining hours, I had set the intention on when I wanted to complete the required clinical hours. Then it came to me, what if there are others in need of clinical hours and entrepreneur training? I would need to get licensed in multiple states to be of any value to these clinical professionals. There was only one problem. I didn't know the first steps in launching and running a business. In school, I was not taught how to start a business, only how to pile up debt and work for someone else forever. Then it came to me by watching Linda run her practice. I started studying others who ran their practices and took on a few contractor jobs to build my hours much more quickly and pay attention to the back-end operations of running a clinical practice. I also kept my vision of having my own clinical practice in the basement in view, just like Jason Seaver of the hit 80s sitcom, *Growing Pains*. I thought it was so cool to work from home. I desired to make that dream a reality. During this entire process, I was adding new skills and new knowledge, and developing new relationships during networking events and counseling conferences. I was on the road to building my voice.

What supplemented my desire to obtain my own practice was the fact that I hit a glass ceiling. Most of the clinical programs either maxed in funding and had to lay many of us off, or it required a license for pay increases. One time, Dr. Traci Lynn, Entrepreneur and Jewelry Fashionista preached at my church. She shared her story of triumph and promise when she said she wasn't going to let anyone *"prostitute her gift and talent and calling the shots on her worth."*

Powerful.

She was working a 9 to 5 and brought in lots of money for the company she worked for, only for that company to decide how much to pay her, which was only a fraction at best of what she brought in for them. She took her talent and skills to work, and she created one of the most successful and well-known jewelry lines. It motivated me to really start my own practice.

But How? When? Where?

I was once told, the how and when is not up to me but is reserved to God. I only need to focus on my Why and What.

Powerful person, what is your Why for building your voice? What is it that you foresee in your future that you have yet to build your voice for?

In three years, I completed all licensure requirements while planning to move to Maryland in 2008. I was looking for my very first home and wanted to take advantage of first time home buyer incentives and credits. Ruminating thoughts of, *"Work for yourself, girl! It's time!"* capitalized on my anxiety to step out of my comfort zone and work for myself. I desired to run my clinical practice since 2003, but the fear of the unknown was the only thing holding me back from entirely building my voice. I then thought of you. Seriously. You were in my heart the entire time. I needed to go through this journey and get my license and write this book simply because of *you.*

Who is in your heart waiting for you to get out of your comfort zone to show up and show out in their lives?

I realized to do all of this, I had to do it afraid. I also needed to reframe my mindset and look at the endless possibilities and the think, what if it does actually work. There is a saying, if your dreams don't scare you, you aren't dreaming big enough. So dream big!

Lastly, I had to accept that God equipped me and provided me with every provision possible to succeed. It was time to do this.

THE EDUCATION

HOW TO BUILD YOUR BUSINESS

Motivational Speaker, Zig Ziglar, said you don't have to be great to start. You just have to start to be great. Have you ever thought about starting your own business but did not know how or where to start? I understand. I was just like you starting off without a clue of which steps to take, and at times being stuck and doing nothing. However, you have a purpose that is bigger, beautiful and beyond you. It is time to learn the fundamentals of building your voice by way of building your business platform. Start building your voice by first branding yourself.

What is branding?

An article in Forbes Magazine defined branding as a process of differentiating yourself in your market to obtain your goal objectives. It is about positioning yourself to people you wish to work with and serve with your product or service.

Do your marketing analysis. Ninety percent of small business owners fail to sustain their businesses because they did not have a plan or strategy around the basic fundamentals of starting their business the right way. Knowing your market trends, competitors and target audience by way of understanding your WHY for entering business puts you ahead of the game and giving you the competitive edge to succeed in your business.

Competitive Advantage. What is your USP? This stands for your unique selling proposition. What is it about your brand, your product or service that makes you stand out from the rest? What is the problem that you solve for your ideal client?

Brand Name. Choose a name that are action words that demonstrate what is called your brand message, or brand promise, to your audience. In other words, whatever it is that you promise to deliver or help your clients with is what is demonstrated within your brand name. For example, my company's name is LeadHER International. I will lead her to be a leader worldwide. One of my coaching programs is Rock Your Voice, where I help aspiring speakers with a story and a message to share turn their passion into profits, aka, Rock Your Voice.

Core Branding. Create logos that reflect your brand and make sure you are consistent across the board in all of your materials, such as on social media, marketing materials, and handouts.

Online Presence. Speaking of social media, establish your voice and brand online and be consistent in your communication. Be clear and concise in your delivery.

Follow these steps in building your voice, and you will become an authority in your desired market of people you wish to serve, as well as creating a platform to overall speak your voice to the masses through your service, product, or program.

THE CONVERSATION
LIFE LESSONS

I had to learn how to build my voice in the clinical space. I was thoroughly equipped to launch my clinical practice and run my business on my own terms. My hang up was not having an example of how to run my business. *Or so I thought.* I was too busy looking at my upbringing and my family for successful entrepreneurs as opposed to looking at entrepreneurs who were in my life. Linda, my supervisor, was an entrepreneur. My friend

Darnyelle, was an up and coming business coach launching her business around the same time as I was. She would also play a part in my transition to business and leadership coaching. I was jealous of how she would make hundreds of thousands of dollars in coaching clients, while I struggled to collect 5 dollar copays in counseling clients. This was a defining moment for me.

I learned to look at what I have and not focus so much on what I do not have. I recognized the possibility of self- sabotaging, or recreating scenarios that thwart my progress, and I had to reframe my thinking to focus on the bigger picture.

You.

I applied for licensure and planned on taking my boards in Maryland. It was a four-hour exam, for which I studied, prayed and praised God in advance for months until the day I arrived to perform.

As I looked for a place to sit and get comfortable for the boards, I sat next to this young lady who said she was on her third round of attempting to pass this exam. I immediately told her, "Best wishes to you," and then I, sure enough, moved somewhere else because I wasn't going to sit next to someone who couldn't pass tests! I didn't want that type of energy near me to retake this exam. That exam cost too much money and too many hours to retake again. My intention was set to make this exam a one and done deal.

That was a long four hours of my life. There were hours when I was tired, hungry, flustered, worried, anxious, you name it. But what kept me going?

Take a moment to look in the mirror. I'll wait.

In the Bible there is a passage that discusses how *Jesus died on the cross for our sins, bearing the shame because of the joy that was set before Him. That joy before Him was us.* Now, I'm no preacher, but I'm making the point that you were my joy that was set before me when I was taking that exam. I had set my intention to build my identity, to build my voice at this point and to let nothing stop me from being able to finally meet you and to share my story to help you get set free and to help you speak your voice. If I did not set the intention to take the exam who knows if our paths would have ever crossed.

I was the last one to complete the boards in four hours. I packed up, drove home to Philly, and waited. That was a long four weeks. The following month, I was coming in from work, and my mom told me there was a letter on my bed. I went to my bedroom and saw the letter from the *National Board of Certified* Counselors. I sat on the bed as I watched the letter. It looked at me, and I looked at it. After a while, I said, *"You know what, Sarah, there's nothing to it but to do it!"* So, I opened up the letter and with one good eye – I had one eye open, and one eye closed just in case I could not take in the entire news that was in that letter– and I scanned it to see whether it was going to say P-A-S-S or F-A-I-L. I squinted my one eye, held my breath, and read out loud P-A-S-S! I started screaming and jumping for joy! I scared my family so bad they thought my screams were a result of a drive-by! I said, "Oh my God, I passed, I passed! I got my license, I got my clinical license!" Everyone started joining in for the celebration. It was such an amazing accomplishment because it meant that my voice was just about built.

I was starting from the beginning; it was almost like a rebirth in a way. There are four cycles of life: *birth, life, death, rebirth.* I was beginning a new path and doing what the Bible suggests; I was forgetting what was behind and focusing on what was ahead.

No longer could I dwell on the sexual assault. It was time to roll up my sleeves and really get down to business in providing efficient, quality clinical psychotherapy for my clients, my very own clients! I was ready to set my mark in this world and ready to speak my voice.

THE REVELATION

TIPS AND RECOMMENDATIONS

Do you forget what has happened to you, so you can start from the beginning or have a rebirth? Or are you stuck in time, still dwelling on the past? Are you swimming in the pain of what has happened to you? Are you still the victim? Here are some tips to help you build your voice:

- ✓ Have someone like a professional counselor to talk to, that can help you through what has happened to you so that you two can brainstorm and work through your challenges. Your current issues may be the result of unaddressed trauma. You do not need to be stuck or in pain any longer. You can start again and have your rebirth. NOTE: If there are any kind of issues that the therapist recommends medication, it is ok. Adequate use of medication helps to stabilize you while using talk therapy to work through your problems effectively and efficiently.

✓ Journaling is also healthy. Journaling is particularly useful for any time that you have reoccurring thoughts, flashbacks, or PTSD symptoms when you find yourself reliving the same trauma over and over and over again. Write out these feelings and experiences.

✓ Build your tool chest of coping skills to help you manage and get over obstacles of any kind.

✓ Support groups are a plus because you are surrounded with like minded individuals who can help encourage and empower you during your building your voice process.

✓ Find a mentor and an accountability partner who can provide direction and guidance to you and hold you accountable for fulfilling your goals to build your voice so that you can ultimately speak your voice.

Build your voice so that you become a significant contributor to making this world a better place for all to speak their voices.

SELF REFLECTION EXERCISE

To **BUILD** Your Voice, get into a quiet space, and give yourself 15-30 minutes to do this exercise. Reflect, free associate, and write down your first thoughts that come to mind when answering the questions below without questioning or altering your answers.

Rewrite The Narrative: If given the opportunity to rewrite your story, what would be different? How would you want your story to be like?

_____
_____
_____

Who do you forgive? What is the wrong for which you are forgiving? Write them down here:

_____
_____
_____

What do you forgive yourself for? List what you regret and what you are willing to forgive yourself here:

_____
_____
_____

Which tip will you employ? Building tool chest, journal, or seek professional services, etc. and how? What is your overall goal in employing any of these tips?

_____
_____
_____

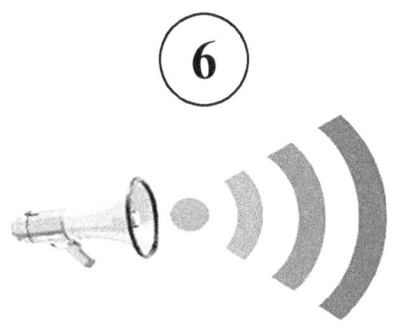

HEAR YOUR VOICE

LISTEN MORE TO YOUR NEEDS

"You will never find peace of mind until you listen to your heart."

– George Michael.

Sarah Renee Langley

MY NARRATIVE

P-A-S-S-E-D! I passed my exam! Whew! What a relief! I am now a Licensed Clinical Professional Counselor for the state of Maryland. So, the next question I had for myself was, *"Now what? What do I do next?"* God has a sense of humor. The year I received my license was around the same time any job I had either closed due to lack of funding or I was fired. Yes, fired. It's nothing like being fired that will set fire to your tail to go out and hustle like never before.

At this time, I was praying and trusting in God for where to run my clinical practice. This was also the time I found out my sweet mom, Mary, was diagnosed with early-onset Alzheimer's Disease. Therefore, it was a lot going on during this time period. I attended church regularly, looking for answers and building my faith for direction and guidance from God. One day during church, I didn't feel well. I went to my car and laid down. My breasts ached. One of the elders checked on me as he watched me abruptly leave service to lay down in my car. I informed him I would be ok and that I needed to make an appointment to see my doctor. I couldn't afford insurance, so I went to the free clinic in my neighborhood. My favorite doctor, whom I had since I was a teenager, was on vacation and her relief was a male doctor. The pain was uncomfortable and concerning since this was my first time experiencing pain in my breast, so I decided to see this male doctor.

When I went in for my appointment and was taken into the examination room, I was instructed to remove my shirt and bra. The pain was in my right breast; there was a lump there. The doctor not only examined my right breast but also my left one to *"justify and compare"* to see if there were any lumps in my left breast. I told him there were none on that side.

As he proceeded with the full breast exam, it felt so uncomfortable because of how he was conducting it. I was by myself with him in the room They didn't have nurses in the rooms with the physicians at this clinic, so again, it was just him and me. I felt as if he was fondling my breasts. But I didn't say anything. *I muted my voice.*

At the end of the exam, he told me that I was a gorgeous young woman and that if I have ever thought of being a model, he had a roommate who was a photographer who would take pictures of me. Further, he offered that should I ever want to get into the modeling business, I could always come to their home to discuss. He gave me his personal pager number and told me that if at any time I wanted to connect with him or with his roommate photographer, I should just call him.

WTF? How in the world does a doctor get away with this? What in the world?

Instead of me going out and reporting him for his incredibly inappropriate behavior, I didn't. I questioned my interpretation as if I was reading too much into this, if this was the norm and he tells all of his beautiful young patients what he told me. I started minimizing my feelings as yet another defense mechanism to avoid the pain and embarrassment, and I had done what I do best.

Criticize myself:

"What did I do to give him that impression? What did I give off? Did I give him a look? Did I poke my breasts out more? Did I give any signals to have him think that I was interested? Did I flash him with my high beams?"

He was supposed to be my doctor, but he had taken advantage of the situation, like someone else I know some years before. So I didn't tell anyone.

Besides, who would believe me, remember?

I decided to handle it myself by reverting back to my male persona. I would defend and protect myself at all costs since the *males in my life weren't going to protect me.*

I wondered how many other girls were going through this same dilemma. I wondered if I should hear my voice within that said <u>*say something.*</u> I was back at the crossroad again where time froze. If I say something and I am *wrong* in my interpretation of the situation, what happens? If I say something and I am right in my interpretation, what happens? I became overwhelmed with it all and had to make a decision if I would report or just not go back there again. Yet, my breasts were the issue. Plus, I did not have any insurance to cover any medical costs. I didn't know what to do. So I did nothing. I decided not to hear my voice and be on mute once again. I *chose* to suffer in silence.

SPEAK YOUR VOICE

Why? I thought more about him than me. I selfishly did not think about you or the countless others that would go through what I went through in the exam room because I did not speak my voice.

One time, I worked as a service coordinator about 5 years before, and I was tasked to do an internal investigation at a workshop for individuals with mental and physical disabilities. Evidence was piling up on the accused regarding misconduct to one of the consumers and I remember talking this over at home with my brothers, and they said, "Wow, you are going to cost that person their job over *misunderstandings?*"

Pause.

The very thing that burns me up in this world is lack of accountability and misplaced responsibility. I believe that for far too long perpetrators, mainly men, have been giving a slap on the wrist if at all for their actions while victims paid the price for such incredulous behavior. Women had to learn how to endure through suffering. Yet, many women supplement this pattern by saying, *"Men aren't mentally strong like us and are like weak little puppies that we must nurture and protect."* In fact, the habit of becoming the men's mommas than significant others blow my mind. We don't seem to have a balance with our nurturing ways. Moreover, we would endure the repercussions of not saying anything than saying something even when it costs us our livelihood. If that is the case, then we prove Mrs. Obama right.

Not only are our voices not important to them, but it is also not important to us.

THE EDUCATION

WHY SEXUAL ASSAULT GOES UNREPORTED

According to the National Sexual Violence Resource Center, one in five women will be raped at some point in their lives. One in five women is sexually assaulted while in college. Ninety-one percent of rape victims in the U.S.A is female, with forty-five percent of men reporting sexual violence but not sexual harassment. Eight percent of rapes occur while the victim is at work.

Rape is the most underreported crime with 63% of sexual assaults not reported to the police, and 90% of college campus assault victims do not report. As a society, we pay more attention to false reporting which is only a whopping 2% to 10%. Maybe we pay more attention to false reporting as a way of deflecting from the real reporting, and to inevitably keep this cycle of rape without reporting it going. A Cosmopolitan magazine survey reported that one in three female employees said they have been sexually harassed at work, with 71% never reporting it. Unfortunately, only 15% felt that the situation was relatively handled.

Here's the thing. Why isn't sexual assault, harassment, and misconduct reported? Why is it that forty or more years later, women are coming forth and alleging that Bill Cosby had sexually assaulted or inappropriately touched them? How is it that these women allowed time to go by and not report? I even questioned the reasons for the #metoo and #timesup movement, when I perceived these movements as having interest in revenge and punishment for *alleged* crimes, crimes that were yet investigated, without looking at how the victims took the deal not to report for the sake of fame and fortune.

And boy, was I so wrong.

I was doing what many others do, comparing false reporting to accurate reporting regarding rape accusations. We tend to look at the problems instead of the benefits of anything that could potentially work to remedy the problem. We look at the possibilities of movements, initiatives, groups, individuals and organizations causing more harm than not. We need to keep things simple and keep everything in its proper context so that the lines are not blurred, and therefore nothing gets done or worse, the problem gets worse.

Here is why sexual assault, harassment, and misconduct goes unreported. According to RAINN, a U.S. anti-sexual violence organization, Twenty percent feared retaliation, 13% believe the police wouldn't do anything, and 13% thought it was personal and therefore didn't want anyone to know. Additionally, 8% thought it wasn't necessary to report, and 7% didn't want to get the perpetrator in trouble.

Therefore, it is a misconception that most victims are choosing not to share their stories because they are getting paid under the table to keep quiet. On the contrary, many do suffer in silence and their stories left untold for reasons just revealed by stats and figures.

Now, the question becomes, *what to do next?* If you are not helping to bring about solutions, you are part of the problem. You may ask, *"Well, what can I do?"* Simple. *Speak Your Voice.*

Share your story or others' stories to stimulate education, conversation and revelation of next steps to end all isms and make this world a better place to live. Support the #metoo movements out there and focus not on the hang-ups but on the good. These movements help countless victims speak their voices. Additionally, become more conscious and empathetic to each other's current challenges as a way to help bring their stories to light. An article in the New York Times talked about how active listening, validating experiences and honoring the feelings of rape and trauma victims are great first steps to making change happen. Lastly, advocacy and commitment to learning and understanding such experiences to push for policy changes also contribute to making lives better for those impacted by sexual assault, harassment, and misconduct.

Your part is to start speaking your voice. Everything else will fall into place when you show up and Speak. Your. Voice.

THE CONVERSATION
LIFE LESSONS

I had a lot to face in deciding to keep quiet or speak up about the male doctor. I chose to stay quiet and handle him myself. It was recommended that I have the lump in my right breast aspirated and checked for any developing cancer. After the procedure and appropriate recovery time, I had to return to the office for a follow-up visit and have the male doctor check my *one breast out* to make sure there were no more lumps. When I returned for the follow-up, the male doctor started to examine me again, going from my right breast to the left. This time I called him out and asked why he was checking on my left breast when it was fine. I told him, *"Don't go over there! You only have to focus on the right!"* Oh my gosh! I did it!

I spoke my voice!

And it shook him up. I saw the reaction on his face. I called him on what he was doing. No, I may not have told other people about what he was doing, but *I spoke my voice.* His voice cracked. He stuttered, and he couldn't stay focused on the exam. He, in a matter-of-fact voice, stated, "Get dressed," and left the exam room. I sat there for a minute, playing what just happened back in my mind. *I spoke my voice, that's what happened!* I thought, *"If that's all it took I should have said something before!"* For that moment, I realized that *I am not helpless. All hope is not lost. I don't have to have things happen to me.* This moment gave me courage and conversely reinforced my decision to be a guy and speak up for myself more often. Sadly, I equated speaking up as *male-oriented, while keeping quite as female-oriented.*

Upon checking out of the clinic, the nurse said she forgot to take my vitals. She had taken vitals and asked me to get up on the scale. The scale was off by 5 lbs. As I stepped off the scale and the nurse went to find paper to write down my vitals, he came towards me, and I informed him their scale was broken as an FYI. He said, "Well, you know where all that weight is going to, don't you? Shocked again, I said, "Where?" He pointed right at my behind! I shook my head and left.

My real doctor returned, and I was tempted to tell her what happened. Evidently, she must've had an idea about him because she wanted to advise me that the male doctor was no longer there because of some things that were said about him.

This entire experience told me we have work to do. I am glad someone spoke their voice. However, I thought about others who have been in the same predicament and wondered what they have done to remedy this problem.

Have you ever been in this situation? Maybe not with a doctor, but with someone that usurp their authority and power to gain at your expense? What did you do? What did you think? What did you say? Was it favorable or unfavorable? Are you ok? Did you write or speak about it? If not, it's high time that you do.

THE REVELATION
TIPS AND RECOMMENDATIONS

If you are stuck and you can't hear your voice, or you lost your voice along the way, stop, take a breath, give thanks that it's not too late to talk about it, and speak your voice.

SPEAK YOUR VOICE

- ✓ Get in a safe, quiet place with your eyes closed and meditate on hearing your voice and listen to what your inner self is saying to you. Your heart is speaking to you; your spirit is talking to you. It will make such a world of difference in your life to help you get free and to help others get free also.
- ✓ Know that you have a better and deeper understanding concerning what you have experienced, whatever the issue or circumstance. You get it, and therefore you will get those who have gone through the same thing because you were once there. This may be your calling to speak your voice about your life lessons, *so prepare!*
- ✓ Build your confidence by getting clear of what your inner voice is saying so that you can put to practice discerning your needs and the needs of others.
- ✓ Trust and respect your inner voice by listening and adhering to it. Trust your gut. It doesn't lie.
- ✓ Celebrate your wins whenever you hear your voice and take action, small or significant. Celebrate anytime you hear and speak your voice.

The most important thing is listening to your inner self and paying attention to what your voice says. Go with it. Your voice within will never steer you wrong.

Sarah Renee Langley

SELF REFLECTION EXERCISE

To **HEAR** Your Voice, get into a quiet space, and give yourself 15-30 minutes to do this exercise. Reflect, free associate, and write down your first thoughts that come to mind when answering the questions below without questioning or altering your answers.

Tell me a time when your voice spoke to you and you disregarded your voice. What was the reason you gave a death ear to your voice?

_____
_____
_____

Close your eyes. Take 3 deep breaths. Inhale, hold, and exhale 3 times. Then write down, what your voice is saying. Free Associate. No right or wrong. Write.

_____
_____
_____

If you had an opportunity to create your own initiative or movement, what would it be called? What would it be about and the solution to the problem it solves?

_____
_____
_____

Write down at least one success regarding steps you had taken to hear your voice and you listened and adhered:

_____
_____
_____

SPEAK YOUR VOICE

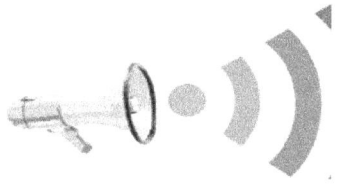

INTERLUDE #3
SARAH, ME TOO

Have you ever carried a secret that was so heavy it felt like you were about to tumble to the ground because of its weight?

Go back in time with me for a moment to the summer of 1982. I was the tender age of seven years old, still young and not mature enough to make any decisions on my own. I loved to play hopscotch, marbles, jacks and fix my baby doll's hair. For the most part, I was a happy child. I loved sweets and would often sneak cookies out of my mother's cookie jar.

One day, as I was taking my usual 2-3 cookies out of the cookie jar, I got caught for the first time by my father. He called me to him, and I thought for sure I was about to get my butt spanked because I knew right from wrong well enough to know that taking those cookies without permission was wrong. When you are a child, you look to your parents primarily for the cues to what you are to say, do and ultimately be. You look to your parents for protection and love. So, when I got caught with the cookies for the first time, it was also the first time that I can remember that my father touched me inappropriately. From that experience, I was molested over the next 6 years. Over those years I repeatedly heard, "This is our secret; don't tell your mother."

After coming to the revelation that what was happening between my father and me was wrong, I could not find the words to tell that this was happening to me. I carried this shameful, painful and embarrassing secret for most of my life. As I was coming into my late thirties, I began mentoring young ladies in high school, college and even some women who were in their 30's, 40's and 50's who had not dealt with different traumatic situations in their past. While mentoring the younger girls, I shared with them that God had called me to write a book about what happened to me as a child. It was in that moment of sharing with the young ladies that I found my voice. One of the young ladies had expressed to me that what had happened to me had happened to her. She went on to say that she knew that she would never be able to stand on stages or open platforms to share her story the way that I was. She asked me to please do her a favor and write the hell out of my book for her and all of those who would never be able to share openly what had happened to them. Without hesitation, I made her that promise. I want to give a voice to the silence that looms around sexual abuse. I want to destroy the walls of secrecy. I wish every little girl who has ever been touched inappropriately by a father, uncle, older brother, a mother's boyfriend or whoever, to know that it was not her fault and that she is not alone. Not only will she get through it and survive but that she will too thrive to heights of greatness. I want every girl or woman to know that her voice has the power. Power to say no, stop, and, ultimately, tell someone in authority what's happening. That she can say, "Yes,

SPEAK YOUR VOICE

this happened to me, but I am not going to let it destroy me."

For me, I carried the secret around for way too long. I now want to encourage those who have heard the repeated phrase of, "What goes on in this house stays in this house," to say with me boldly and confidently - "NOT ANYMORE!"

-Lady Joy

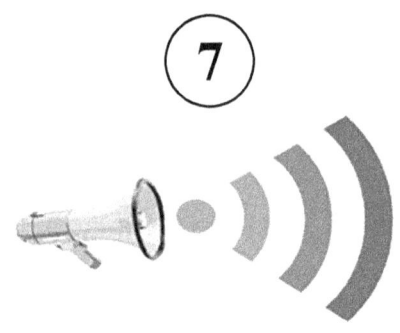

LOVE YOUR VOICE

EMBRACE YOU

"Embrace yourself, accept and love yourself, and you will shine brighter."

PINAY.COM

SPEAK YOUR VOICE
MY NARRATIVE

So he had pointed right to my behind to say that all of my weight went right there as I was leaving his office. *The nerve of him!* I just finished shutting him down in the exam room for fondling my breasts, like I wasn't aware of what he was doing.

I heard my inner voice say loud and clear *"Speak your voice!"*

I was so happy I did.

Then the next question for myself was, *"What's next? Now what?"*

Have you ever used the fan to distort your voice? When I was a little girl, my brother Jon and I would sit in front of the fan and feel the fresh air blowing in our faces. We would make this sound through the fan that would change up our voices. It would either echo or create a vibration, and we thought that was so cool hearing our voices change and project like that. We had a great time. We were so amazed to hear our voices through the fan. I *liked my voice back then.*

As an adult, however, I'll admit I hadn't liked my voice, literally and figuratively. I hadn't like my laugh, my tone, or the way I spoke. I was not in love with my voice at all. At one point, I was amazed by my voice, but after the rape, I started to no longer love my voice. Maybe because of the way I perceived my voice as being insignificant in this world since then. It seemed negligible to many, so eventually, I just stopped loving my voice.

Why would I think that my voice was significant anyway? How could I have when I learned how to sacrifice my time and needs for the sake of others? In the name of setting the captives free through my clinical practice, I sacrificed my self-care for everyone else's needs and for two reasons. First, I thought it was the Christian thing to do, and second, I was taught to do so as a clinical counselor.

In counseling, therapists follow the medical model just like hospitals; we can't turn you away if you don't have money. We have sixteen codes of ethics to conform to. One of the codes is about remuneration. If the client could not pay, we were to serve him or her anyway. So mainly, we had to write our services off in the name of helping our fellow men and women fix their problems. Some therapists had to go home to the threat of lights being turned off, homes going into foreclosure, or cars being repossessed. It was as if we were unimportant in comparison to our clients AND in favor of managed care. As an independent contractor for other group practices, I accepted the *'usual and customary'* terms of managed care for clients who used their medical insurance for counseling. This meant that once again, someone was calling the shots on my life. I wasn't working for myself, I still worked for the man who dictated my worth and value by way of compensation, or lack thereof.

With my life feeling like an emotional rollercoaster, I started to forget the goal I had in establishing my very own private practice. I started to forget about the hard work I had put in to start my business. In my basement. Just like Jason Seaver.

SPEAK YOUR VOICE

After I received my clinical license, I had to find a place to set up shop and see clients. I applied on panels with insurances for my practice so I could initially obtain clients. I was a Mental Health Director at a correctional facility and befriended a colleague named Dan. We quickly hit it off, and I shared with him how I was in the process of looking for a home with a finished basement to conduct my counseling practice. I prayed, set the intention and focused on what I wanted. I hired a real agent named Gaynelle who helped me search for the right home. I was thoroughly excited for both my very first home and business simultaneously happening. We found the perfect home that had everything I wanted because I was intentional. I prayed and knew what I wanted in my heart and mind. I saw what I wanted before it visually manifested. I would drive to the parking space and sit there looking at the home, once in the morning as if I was leaving from there and once at night as if I was coming home. I pictured my clients coming there and my schedule booked to capacity. My dreams initially came to a halt when I found out I was only approved for so much money towards the home. I asked Gaynelle if the sellers would consider accepting the amount offered. She thought that was a daring move and strongly felt they would not accept my request. She did find another lender who provided a little bit more money, but it was not close to the asking price.

Yet, I did not waver.

Gaynelle was also a Christian believer, and we prayed together for favorable decisions concerning the buying price. I need this home. I have to help people speak their voices, so it has to go in my favor.

Gaynelle called me and said if I was sure that I wanted to move forward and ask the sellers to accept my offer. I said yes. All we can do is ask. I stood in certainty, that was my home. Another daring move was me visiting the home and talking with the sellers. They were so impressed with me and my intentions for the house, they felt it was the right fit. A few days later, Gaynelle calls me.

"I don't believe it! They said yes! In my 10 years of doing real estate, I have never seen sellers accept so low of what they were asking!"

I loved the fact that I spoke up and just asked. You never know when it may be your yes day, so ask and see which way it goes. However, we weren't out of the woods. I had to come up with 6200 dollars in closing costs! *Wow*! I thought. I had enough faith to get them to accept my offer, and now I have to have more faith to come up with $6200! I asked myself, "How bad do I want my dream to come to past?" I continued praying and setting the intention to close on my Jason Seaver house.

One day, when I had talked to Dan over lunch, he asked how it was going regarding closing on the home. I informed him I was only short by $6200 in closing costs.

What happens next shocked me, and located more of my automatic thoughts.

"Ms. Sarah, if you need it, I can give it to you."

"What? Give me what?"

"I can give you the money Ms. Sarah, not a problem." (MUTE)

"Ms. Sarah?"

My automatic thoughts were as follows:

"What's does he want? Do I need to sleep with him, because I am NOT doing that! Should I sleep with him? Why in the world is he offering me all of this money? Should I take it? We just met!"

"Ms. Sarah? What do you say?"

"Let me get back to you Dan."

It is interesting that we tend to be surprised when what we asked for comes to past! It can happen however way it happens, but as long as it happens and you're ready for it, *accept it!*

I accepted it. What I also noticed was my *stinkin' thinkin'*. Apparently, Dan and others loved my voice more than I. They saw the value I brought not only to the inmates but to the staff at the prison. I had a message to share what brought joy to many and contention to others because of how I carried myself with confidence. My license afforded me to quickly get promoted to Mental Health Director and supervise staff who has worked in the mental health unit for years. What seemed doom and gloom when my professor failed me afforded me the opportunity and upward mobility.

Thanks, Dr. White!

Somewhat off topic, there was one slight challenge I wanted to address. The fact that I was privy to everyone's pay and noticed that during pay negotiations, I went up $5000, but an inexperienced non-licensed male counselor came in during my probationary period as Mental Health Director and he was granted only $1000 less than me! The mental health unit was predominately women, and their pay scale was much less, although they have worked in the unit longer than me and the guy. The inequality was real, and I started speaking my voice on it. I realized I had a heart of advocacy for fairness and justice. I understood my voice was needed in so many ways, and the doors were opening for me to speak my voice in my own clinical practice.

One significant discovery I had was that I lacked self-care. Often, I was tired, burned out, maxed out and stressed out. It was becoming tumultuous at home with mom suffering from Alzheimer's disease and the impact it had on my brothers and me. All kinds of pent-up emotions and animosities came out toward one another. We were hurt and scared to lose our best friend to this disease, and we didn't know the first thing about what to do. I was also embarking on a new journey as an entrepreneur and business owner in my new home. I'm about to have my own clients, and I was already thinking about opening up an internship program, multiple offices in different states, and starting my doctoral program. BUT, this is what I truly discovered in all of this. *I was avoiding the void in my life*. I still did not get over the rape. I saw how my automatic thoughts were piling up because I never really addressed them.

Have you ever had *unfinished business* to address? I collected achievements and accomplishments along the way that gave me no reason to address my unaddressed issues. But, the rape didn't go away. In fact, when I counseled clients who have experienced rape, I had to always be mindful not to project or transfer my attitudes and beliefs onto my clients in risk of giving them the wrong advice. I thought it was over and I had moved on, but any triggers of people taking advantage of me, not giving me the courtesy to make decisions, or evidence of possibly blindsiding me, resulted in lashing out, getting angry, or verbal aggression. That is why I didn't love my voice. I was still broken, operating with the perfect mask on, avoiding the pain and void I carried since 18. I needed help and fast before I became suicidal. Again.

THE EDUCATION

PTSD AND MDD

After being exposed to a traumatic event, anyone can experience the illness called post-traumatic stress disorder (PTSD). Some of the most common symptoms associated with PTSD are recurrent distressing thoughts, nightmares, and flashbacks about the traumatic event. Those suffering from PTSD often get distressed by sights, smells, and sounds that remind them of the incident. Along with these symptoms, those with PTSD experience alienation, avoidance of people and places, emotional numbing, lack of a sense of future, survivor's guilt, difficulty falling or staying asleep, difficulty concentrating or remembering, hyper-vigilant or survivalist behavior, and exaggerated startle response, particularly to loud and unexpected noises.

Major Depression

While everyone experiences feelings of sadness throughout his or her life, major depression is defined as a mental disorder in which a person experiences such strong and long-lived feelings of sadness, anxiety, hopelessness, guilt, helplessness, etc. that it interferes with his or her everyday life. Like other mental illnesses, depression is caused by a chemical imbalance in the brain. This imbalance can be caused by hereditary factors, medical problems, a variety of unpleasant experiences, and even certain personality traits. Depression is not limited to mental symptoms, however; it also affects physical health and wellbeing. Psychological symptoms include thoughts of death or suicide, feelings of sadness and emptiness, irritability, and difficulty concentrating and/or remembering. Those experiencing depression can experience a loss of interest or joy in activities they once enjoyed, insomnia or excessive sleep, significant weight loss or gain, and chronic pain without improvement with treatment. Those suffering from depression can experience any of these symptoms but do not have to possess all of the symptoms associated with the disorder to be legitimately diagnosed with major depression.

Treatment Options

When one is ready to overcome it to reset his or her life, it is essential to consider the various treatment options available. Psychotherapy is a possible treatment option. One can either enter into individual or group therapy. Group therapy, for example, often gives the clients a feeling that they are not alone in facing their struggles. Others in the group will have similar experiences as you and may be at different stages in the recovery process. Therefore, they could potentially give you another perspective on their personal experience. Group therapy may be particularly helpful for those struggling with communication problems (i.e., those suffering from a social phobia). Individual treatment, on the other hand, offers other positives to the person seeking treatment. Firstly, there is a greater sense of confidence; only the therapist will have access and knowledge of your personal information and secrets. There is also more attention paid to the individual person and their struggles which often allows for the therapist and client to go deeper into the issues at hand. Finally, you are able to arrange your own time; you do not have to coordinate your schedule with other members of the group. There is no right answer for which kind of therapy is best for you, to achieve the best outcome, you must decide what you want from your therapy session in the long run. Medication management may also be an essential part of a treatment plan you might consider. If you and your therapist decide that medication would help to improve your condition, it is important to periodically check in with your psychiatrist to document your progress and to make any changes that may be necessary.

Do you believe psychotherapy and support services are in order after learning about PTSD and MDD? *There is no such thing as a weakness, only uncultivated strengths waiting for its opportunity to transform. Seeking help is ok. Seeking help is a strength.*

THE CONVERSATION
LIFE LESSONS

As humans, we are comprised of three things: mind, body, and spirit. You may or may not believe in a higher power, but one thing is for sure – you do have a spirit, a soul. We can attend to our minds all day long, but if we do not attend to our body and spirit, we are not considered a whole self. We can attend to our body, but if we do not attend to our mind and spirit, we are not considered a whole self. We can attend to our body and mind, but if we do not attend to our spirit, we are still not considered a whole self.

Let me ask you a question because, again, powerful people ask powerful questions:

Are you whole? Do you feel complete? Isn't it time to shift gears and start caring even the more about yourself and love your voice?

With all that was going on, from starting my business to closing on my home to contention between my brothers and me, to mom's decline with Alzheimer's Disease, to the effects of the rape, *I was stressed out*. Before I get any worse, I decided to go to counseling. As therapists, we were encouraged to seek therapy while counseling so that our personal matters do not interfere with advising our clients. Actually, there's a running joke about counselors. Have you heard it before? The reason why we become counselors is that we have our own issues we can't fix, so we end up trying to fix you instead! Don't misunderstand me, it is a strength to recognize your weaknesses and to admit there is a problem to work through so that you can be healthy and whole.

But I'm just sayin'.

When I was seeing Doris, I felt freer. I was able to let my guard down in therapy. I realized I had trust issues and that my heart was calloused. More automatic thoughts included, *"You are innocent until proven guilty, but you only have one shot at being innocent. Mess that up, and you wind up in my mistrust file forever."* Amazingly, I've helped my clients through mistrust, trauma, and other challenges, yet I couldn't fix my own. I felt embarrassed, disappointed, and ashamed.

Doris helped me open up about my physical abuse at 13, the rape at 18, and my contentious relationship with my dad and brothers. I was quite intense in therapy and verbally aggressive when I brought up trigger points that set me off. For insurances purposes, Doris diagnosed me with Generalized Anxiety Disorder. Doris helped me peel back the layers of my life to get to the core issues. The defining moment for me in counseling was when I discovered something I didn't realize. I discovered that I did not love myself. I did not love my voice. My main core automatic thought was, *"I am unlovable."* And it did not stem from the rape or the abuse.

It originated from the relationship with my dad.

Based on the relationship I had with my dad, I formulated a philosophy of how males see females. For me, I knew that my dad loved me, but I didn't think that he cared for me too much because of our interactions. He seemed distant and emotionally unavailable. *Little girls need love and attention from their dads.* In therapy, I realized that I had a significant problem with unfairness and injustice because I saw the difference between the regard he had for my brothers and the little regard he had for me. My dad had this Southern Old School mentality that boys were much more valuable and regarded than girls.

I had significant breakthroughs in therapy. With Doris' help, I began removing the callous from my heart so that I can love my voice. I realized just because others do not love me doesn't mean I need to follow suit. I needed to love me. The more you allow yourself to process your thoughts and feelings, preferably with a counselor, friend or confidant, even through journaling, the freer you become. We tend to be politically correct and mind our P's and Q's on what we say so that we don't hurt anyone's feelings. However, when you free associate, which is an analytical process in saying whatever comes to your heart or mind, profound breakthroughs occur. I want you to experience your breakthrough.

Take the limits off. No holds barred.

When I finally free associated with Doris, the most profound thing happened. She simply asked, "How do you think your father thinks of you?" Without thought, the word naturally came out of my mouth- *Defective*.

Right after I said this word, it felt like an enormous boulder rolled off of me! Instantly, I cried and cried and cried.

If you are crying right now or felt to cry, it's ok. Please give yourself permission to cry. If anything in this book touches you and brings you to tears, please do not stop yourself from letting the tears flow. When was the last time you had a good cry? Do you know what crying is? Crying is just another way of speaking when you verbally cannot. Your words are in your tears, which that immediately opens the door for healing, peace, and clarity. Doris helped me to see that I cannot measure my value and worth by my dad's measuring stick but by my own measuring stick. I cannot measure my value and worth based on the measuring sticks of all the guys I slept with, but by my own measuring stick. I cannot measure my value and worth based on my virginity or opinions of others. My value and worth are not predicated on my actions and behaviors. My value and worth are based on my truth of *who I am*.

The question was, *Who Am I?* And that's what broke for me. I had a clean slate, a rebirth, an exciting journey ahead of me on discovering who Sarah Renee Langley is. It was a journey I so looked forward to now that I buried what I call the Triple Ds:

distractions, defeats, and dead weight. I was now able to learn how to love my voice.

Powerful person, let me ask you these powerful questions: *Do you love your voice? Are you waiting for someone to love and regard you?* Please don't. For everyone to love and respect you, you first have to love and respect yourself. Show the world how to treat you so they can follow suit. Know that your value and worth is based on coming to know who you truly are. I dare you to take that journey of learning who you are to become. It is an awesome one, filled with hope, promise, opportunity, and freedom.

It is time to love your voice.

THE REVELATION
TIPS AND RECOMMENDATIONS

Loving your voice plays as a piece of the puzzle to making this world a better place to live. It is a matter of self-actualizing and not discarding or rejecting the attributes you believe are unacceptable to others. You must set the tone and be the first one to love your voice. Love your voice first. Here's how:

- ✓ **Learn more about yourself.** Dedicate 15 minutes to mediating and reflecting on who you are and what you bring to the table of life. How do play a part in making the world a better place to live?
- ✓ **Recondition your mindset.** Take the time to learn your

automatic thoughts and unspoken rules. Knowing your thoughts and feelings will position you to take hold of them and replace any *stinkin' thinkin'* with positive thoughts about yourself.

- ✓ **Challenge yourself** by asking others what makes you lovable. Ask them what it is about you that stands out. Ask them to describe you in one word.
- ✓ **Set higher expectations** for yourself and make it a point to connect with those who you deem are more advanced and faster than you.
- ✓ **Start embracing** every single single part of you and appreciate your quirky, silly ways.

Setting the example on how to love your voice gives permission to others to love their voices.

SELF REFLECTION EXERCISE

To **LOVE** Your Voice, get into a quiet space, and give yourself 15-30 minutes to do this exercise. Reflect, free associate, and write down your first thoughts that come to mind when answering the questions below without questioning or altering your answers.

What do you find unlovable about yourself and why?

_____
_____
_____

What attributes others tend to love about you?

_____
_____
_____

What are the past or current Triple Ds- Distractions, Defeats and Dead Weights in our life that you know you must let go of? What had you to hold on to these?

_____
_____
_____

Write down 7 things that you love yourself for and recite them daily for the next 30 days.

_____
_____
_____

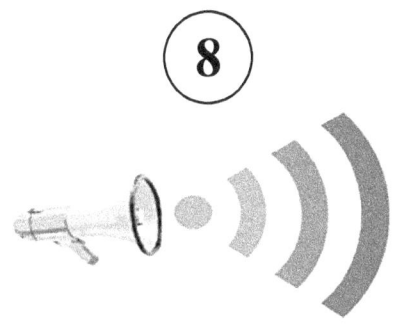

SHOW YOUR VOICE

DEMONSTRATE

"Don't compromise yourself – you're all you have."

--John Grisham.

Sarah Renee Langley

MY NARRATIVE

I'm *defective*! I exclaimed to my therapist Doris during my breakthrough moment in our counseling session. I gave such a roar of a cry after I said the word defective as if Pandora's box was unleashed waiting to open up and let out all of its contents that's been pressure cooking since forever and a day. I felt so *free! Liberated! Alive!* That was a huge relief to admit something that I thought I was wrong to feel because after all, I am talking about my hardworking father, who has provided for our family for 50 plus years. How could I talk about my father like that? *Well, I did.* And I was relieved. It actually helped me look at how skewed my view was of him. In fact, years later, I told him about my counseling session and my perception of how he viewed me. He said, *"On the contrary, you are my heart and my world. I thank God for you every day."* I didn't know. It is amazing how a conversation can make a world of difference to get on the same page and understand each other's perspectives. I challenge you to start having relevant conversations with individuals you think have a problem with you and see if your perceptions are correct or not to then take next steps. It is time to bring closure to *unfinished business* and tie up loose ends because now is the time to *show your voice.*

After I closed on my home, I took my new keys, posted them on facebook, sped to my new house, ran all around the empty house screaming for joy, and called my Mom. I yelled in her ear saying, "Mommy can you believe it! YAAAAYYYYYY!" She said, "I am so proud of you! Praise God!" As I cried profusely, I said, "This is a proud moment for both of us mommy!" "That's right baby, just cry it out."

My mom is the best.

After the call, I went to the basement and looked around. I visualized the waiting couch, the desk, the table with magazines, the tv on the wooded built-in entertainment center area, and, of course, the infamous counseling couch in the main room. It was perfect! Then suddenly, people donated sofas, TVs, computers, chairs and other items toward my vision. It was amazing! There is a saying, *you get what you picture.*

I even started receiving client calls. And guess what? I wasn't ready for them! I was scared.

Scared of what, you ask? To demonstrate my voice, of course.

Why, you ask? Because I wanted to be perfect! I wasn't sure if I was actually ready to counsel my own clients for my business. I continued working as an independent contractor for other agencies, but I remembered what Dr. Traci Lynn said at church. I can do this for myself and pocket all the money for my business.

One year after obtaining licensure I turned in my resignation to my contractor jobs and accepted my very first client in my Jason Seaver home.

I treated the client as a guest. I offered him something to drink and asked if he was comfortable on the couch. I was nervous and didn't know what to expect. However, I conducted the therapy session and believed it went well. So well, I received more referrals and therefore, more clients.

In the next few years, I outgrew my home and moved my practice into professional buildings. I established four offices with at least two staff per office, obtaining licensure in almost 8 states. Yes, I was running a successful clinical practice and I loved it. It was awesome to show my voice to my clients and help them show their voices in their situations. I had one young lady who shared that she was recently raped on campus. We discussed how rape is all about dominance and control and how she regains her power by speaking her voice and doing something about it. We explored how it was her choice to report to the police, form a coalition on her campus to help others speak their voices, or do nothing and stay powerless. The young lady said she had such a significant breakthrough moment in our session that she realized she had to demonstrate her voice not only for herself but for other young women and men to contribute to the solution of rape prevention. This moment was momentous for me as I started to accept why life happens to us.

It is for someone else to live.

I was happy. Life couldn't get any better. Until life happened put my happiness to the test.

SPEAK YOUR VOICE

I became the primary caregiver for my mother who now has late-stage Alzheimer's. I wanted to be there for mom in the fullest capacity possible, so I had set the intention to build my administration team and my staff to run my clinical practice. Additionally, I trained aspiring therapists through my internship program to demonstrate how to show their voices in their practices. The internship afforded my counselees the opportunity to not only obtain licensure but to successfully run their own clinical practices.

It was a fantastic ride from where I started to where I had reached. The fact that I could go from the basement in my house to now having multiple offices in multiple states blew my mind. This poor little girl from North Philly who once lost her identity and died was born and renewed again, taking everything that she went through to now show off her new voice. Demonstrating how you, too, can rise to the occasion. You, too, can make it. You, too, can turn your obstacles into opportunities for yourself. I used my challenges and circumstances in a way to prove myself but also to use it to my advantage to shut up the naysayers---to the ones who said I wouldn't make it, to the ones who said, statistically, I should already have five kids by six different baby daddies, on welfare in North Philly. And while this is no shade on anyone whose lifestyle is like that, this is to say you, too, can defy the odds no matter what.

I became confident in my identity and confident in who I was becoming. I was setting the example for others to do the same thing, to be sure of who they are and to demonstrate who they are by showing their voices. With this newfound confidence, I give all praises to God who paved the way for me.

Remember, I did this scared. I didn't know how I was going to get from point A to point B. All I had to concern myself with was my why, and to make sure I was furthering my message, expanding my reach to the masses, so that I simultaneously create the lifestyle I desired and deserved.

Get ready to show your voice.

THE EDUCATION

GOAL SETTING

If you fail to plan, you plan to fail. Do you have goals? Jim Rohn said, "Your goals are in direct correlation to your bank account." If you have goals, are you achieving them? One case study showed that 92% fail to meet their goals compared to the 8% that do. What gives? Why is it only 8% meeting them?

What is goal setting anyway?

Goal setting is a decision of going after what you want to accomplish and creating a plan of action in achieving the results you want. It also helps organize your time, resources and energy to make the most of your life. Researcher Edwin Locke believed that when individuals set challenging goals and dream big, they perform better than those who set basic goals. Why? The more challenging the goal the more rewarding it is. Going after your dreams to turn them into reality is a process that takes skill, discipline, focus, and fortitude It also results in character building and maturity. Taken from my book, It's Your *Turn NOW! 7 Secrets To Living Life On Your Own Terms,* which the full version is available for purchase, or the mini version is available for free at drsarahreneelangley.com, I discuss something called S.I.M.P.L.E. Goals.

S.I.M.P.L.E goals, developed by Rick Torben, were designed for managers to use for their employees. Each letter represents a particular action step to complete for ultimate happiness and success.

Set Expectations. Set your focus, time, energy, and resources toward attaining your happiness and success. Be clear about your own expectations so as to not set yourself up for failure and disappointment. Be realistic and make your goals feasible to attain. If you hope to really start your own business, rearrange your life according to the expectation you have and the goal you wish to fulfill. Examples are setting the expectation to network, research, investing in a business coach, or creating a business plan. Do not expect to start your business if you do not change anything contrary to what kept you from starting your business. Set expectations of yourself, be clear about them, and show yourself the courtesy to follow through on them. Journal your journey and pay attention to any negative self- talk, resistance, feelings, behaviors, and actions. Notate any external distractions, like family or friends, that may actually play against you in accomplishing your goals. You are shifting in your life, and everyone in your life may be comfortable with you remaining the same. But if you are not comfortable, make the necessary shift and arrangements to achieve your goals.

Invite Commitment. Commit to achieving your goals. You may have been very committed to everything else in your life, even committed to being successful, but that does not mean it translates or will transfer over to a commitment for this new personal goal of happiness and success for yourself. Please journal how accomplishing these goals will personally benefit you and how it will benefit others. But the focus should really be on how it benefits you; you have already done things that directly benefited others and indirectly benefited yourself. It is time for this goal to primarily and solely benefit you to fully understand what it is to be happy and successful for yourself, *unapologetically, and guiltlessly*. Give yourself permission to feel good at having this goal being all about you. Additionally, create a way to hold yourself accountable. I will address this later when we get to the **L** in S.I.M.P.L.E.

Measure Progress. Create performance measure to track your progress so that you can determine if you are meeting your goals. Review and assess your performance measure to see the steps you have taken in your attempt to completing this goal. When you track and measure, you can see where you have deviated from your plan, where you fell and where you can tweak your steps to successfully complete your goals. Writing about what happened in your Happiness and Success Journal will also make a world of difference in a few ways. First, you can turn journal into a book for others to know how to become happy and successful. Second, you can refer back to your journal when you face other challenges and see how you were able to triumph and overcome them. Lastly, you have a standard to create future goals.

Provide Feedback. As mentioned in explaining the M in S.I.M.P.L.E., providing feedback regarding your thoughts, feelings, and behavior is crucial because you can explore its source of creation. Your response during this process of pursuing happiness and success for yourself may be noteworthy as it may tell a lot about whether it is the same behavior that was modeled, or if it is a result of your upbringing. Perhaps your mom tried to be happy and attempted to start her own business, but she self-sabotaged or she created problems that interfered with her goals because your dad subconsciously wanted your mom to be dependent on him as head and breadwinner. As a result, she inevitably stopped her attempts to start her business to protect their relationship. Explore if there are similar undertones in your current relationship with your significant other or with others.

Link to Consequences. This is my favorite S.I.M.P.L.E. goal! Why you ask? We are motivated by rewards and consequences. We have learned how to be driven by rewards and consequences since we were young. I learned not to do what my brothers did to avoid punishment. They received enough whippings for all of us! I witnessed which behaviors were rewarded and which behaviors were penalized. I would like for you to create a behavior and thinking chart. Write down all of the positive thoughts, self-sabotaging thoughts, and actions that lead you to your happiness and success, and also list the positive thoughts, self-sabotaging thoughts, and behaviors that take you off course. Once you listed them, then you can create a daily chart for these items so that on a weekly basis you are tracking how you are doing. If you have completed your mini goals in the process of accomplishing your long-term goals, *Celebrate and Reward Yourself!* Create a list of rewards that you can choose from. If you did not complete your mini goals in the process of accomplishing your goals, then link the consequence to it. That means no cell phone for a week except for emergencies. (Be careful what you classify as emergencies so that you don't cheat and use the cell phone for an emergency call to your friend about what happened on Game of Thrones!). It is about maturity and discipline, and if you do not deserve to celebrate your mini successes because you did not meet your goal so far, then you need to have a consequence that you know will propel you to do better next time.

Case Study: Me

I once worked in medical records for a teen summer program called Phil-a-Job in Philadelphia when I was 16. It was my very first professional job, and it was also the very first time I was fired! *Yes, I was getting fired as early as 16. Yeah, I know.* I think it had something to do with me not doing my job as expected. While I had the job, I put a gold ring with my middle name, Renee, on a layaway plan. I went to the jewelry store every two weeks to pay my ring off. I had a goal in mind and that was to have my ring by the end of the summer. But I didn't do my job as expected, and as a consequence, I was fired. You'd think I would have learned from this over the years because I mentioned earlier I was fired and laid off a few more times! I talked my way into getting my job back, and I worked harder than ever. I finally purchased my ring, and I was so happy! When I received my job back, I was motivated to do my job as intended and better than anyone else, which I did. I gave it the respect that the position deserved, and the reward was the respect of the staffs that threw me a party when the summer job ended. The best homemade carrot cake ever! Plus, I was able to wear my beautiful *Renee* ring to the party!

Make sure you link your rewards and consequences to your goals of happiness and success so that you can stay on track and fulfill all your goals. Finally, we come to the E in S.I.M.P.L.E. goals.

Evaluate Effectiveness. Review, assess, and analyze how your journey has been regarding your goals toward happiness and success. As mentioned earlier, notate all that has worked for you and that which has resulted in the fulfillment of your goals, and then discard what has not worked. In other words, *take in the meat and spit out the bones.* Ever heard of that before? For the sake of the point, the meat is the best part, the part that nourishes and helps us to become strong. Therefore, take in what works for your happiness and success and get rid of what doesn't work. Do not make the mistake of copying others' ways of accomplishing goals. What worked for others may not work for you.

I remember telling my couples during relationship counseling that instead of patterning after their parents' marriage, they should only take bits and pieces that they would like to apply to their own marriage. I encouraged them to seize their most significant opportunity in recreating their own style of marriage. Many of them were happy and thankful for this tip on creating change and doing things differently. Likewise, write down what works for you and what doesn't work for you with regards to obtaining your happiness and success. Then, turn it into a how-to book and publish it later on, and then watch it become a best seller! You will be amazed at how your own unique story will significantly impact and make a difference for those going through the same things as you are right now.

THE CONVERSATION

LIFE LESSONS

Let's talk about closure to unfinished business. What do I mean and why is that important? It is important to address so that nothing stands in your way of showing your voice as you journey to ultimately speak it. Remember when I confessed my feelings and perception towards my dad? Once I settled that and brought closure to the situation, I saw other unfinished businesses in my life. I saw how my relationships with guys correlated with my relationship with my dad, the guy who raped me and in my steady relationship with my former boyfriend, Tyrone. Tyrone was 15 years my senior.

Often, unbeknownst to us, we recreate situations that are synonymous with what we have experienced growing up that we didn't have closure. Why? If we could not fix it in one scenario, we will try to fix it in another. We subconsciously recreate the scene in hopes that the outcome is in our favor. What is hurtful and damaging is when the scenario still plays out the same way that it did even when we first experienced it with someone else. It tends to be a dysfunctional cycle and we get stuck, so pay attention to the similarities and the differences between your relationships, your significant other, with your parents, and whoever else.

Tyrone and I dated for ten years until it hit me. There were so many similarities between him and my daddy; he was older than me and a musician, a bassist (my daddy is a guitarist), as well as perceiving him as emotionally unavailable. He was very conservative, quiet and kept to himself. Yes, even as a clinical psychotherapist, I had recreated my own dysfunction and attempted to fix it. The problem is that I could not fix it. *So what was a girl to do?*

Let it go.

Let it go to bring closure to your unfinished business. If the situation is not going in the direction that you want it to go, let it go. By letting the relationship with Tyrone go, it really helped me open my eyes to what attracts me, what I was putting out in the atmosphere on the kind of relationship I desired and the person I wanted to date and what I did not want in a relationship. I realized I still had more work to do to show my voice.

While obtaining my masters, I had taken a group psychotherapy course. Our professor grouped four other ladies with me for this exercise. In the exercise, my professor brilliantly noticed my reactions to trigger words during our group conversations, to which she concluded I struggled with things that are left unfinished. I have a problem with unfinished business. *Eureka*! I thought back to the rape and how I checked out during the heinous act. I never really dealt with it. It was just left unfinished. Even though I told a few people and helped others cope with being raped, I had not worked through the issue for myself. I think at that time it was just too much for me to really go there. I actually thought I was set free from it since having my breakthrough during my counseling session with Doris.

Unfortunately, I still operated as if I was subjugated. Powerful person, here's the powerful question: *What unfinished businesses do you have? What have you left unattended? What have you recreated and have yet to fix the problem?*

Amazingly, with my hang ups and problems, I still counseled others. I still had my masks on. I again showed up significant to others even when I was feeling insignificant alone. I didn't want to deal with the pain of being insignificant and worthless and nothing. I still did not want to address my pain. I developed a habit of perfecting my outward appearance as a tactic to not deal with the war within myself. That was not the voice I wanted to show.

Until.

I realized what I had been through plays a part in showing my voice. I can share a perfect blend of failures and successes, defeats and victories.

To me, t*hat is a real voice.*

I encourage you to do a retrospective look within and see if there are any unfinished business in your life. You really have to do the work to bring closure to one situation so that it helps bring closure to other situations and to be in a position to show what a true voice really is.

Show your voice.

THE REVELATION

TIPS AND RECOMMENDATIONS

To move forward in your life, it is time to bring closure to unfinished business. Here's how.

- ✓ **Honesty.** Be completely honest with yourself as you reflect on your life and see what situations need to end.
- ✓ **Transparency**. Be real about the situation. Do not pretend or act like the situations left unattended never happened. The quicker you address them, the more open doors you will have for a brighter future.
- ✓ **Tell the truth.** Admitting you have had problems in the past that resulted in unfinished business is half the battle won.
- ✓ **Look at the signs.** Look at the similarities and differences between yourself and others and the common theme that leads to unfinished business and avoidance to address them

✓ **Move on.** Now that you have acknowledged and addressed the unfinished business, let it all go and move on.

Bringing closure positions you to show your voice for others to do the same thing.

SELF REFLECTION EXERCISE

To SHOW Your Voice, get into a quiet space, and give yourself 15-30 minutes to do this exercise. Reflect, free associate, and write down your first thoughts that come to mind when answering the questions below without questioning or altering your answers.

What are the unfinished businesses in your life? Why?

_____
_____
_____

What will be your attempt to bring closure to the unfinished businesses?

_____
_____
_____

What is the one thing you will do differently going forward to no longer have unfinished businesses open in your life?

_____
_____
_____

What are the new order of businesses you will concentrate on accomplishing?

_____
_____
_____

SPEAK YOUR VOICE

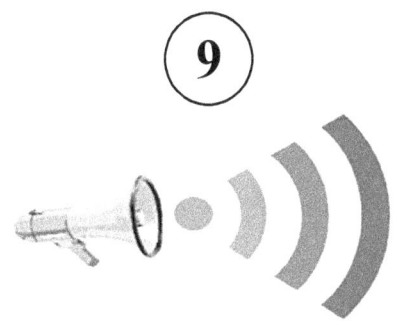

OWN YOUR VOICE

CLAIM IT! POWER

"It's not your responsibility to want the life that others want for you."

Colin Wright.

Sarah Renee Langley

MY NARRATIVE

In the summer of 2014, I was on Facebook and saw an advertisement on the right side of the screen that said something along the lines of, "Do you want to be a millionaire?" I clicked on it. It was an invitation to a conference the organization was having. At that time, I wasn't able to attend.

In February 2015, I saw the same advertisement. I clicked on it, and it said, "Do you want to be a millionaire? Do you want to have a millionaire mind?" I saw it was a free event and said, *"You know what? I want to go to this."* The event was in Baltimore.

I jumped in the car and went and met my assistant Vergie and her husband there. At the conference, the speakers discussed how becoming a millionaire should be an intention. It was absolutely mind-blowing how they talked about the principles of money, having a money mindset, conversations around money, and how it ties in with your purpose.

My life was transformed by attending this free three-day event. By the last day of the event, the host made an offer to the participants that was too difficult to refuse. It was to become a certified coach through their program. It was an opportunity to further my studies surrounding leadership and coaching, so I invested in myself through their program,

I had never looked back since.

Being part of a supportive network afforded me the opportunity to learn who I was and to accept who I was becoming.

I was beginning to define and own my voice. One key ingredient to success is relationship building. People gravitated to me and showed interest in anything I had to say. I felt God's favor resting upon me. It was undeniable. People complimented my looks, style, speech, and aura. People genuinely loved being around me and noted how high my energy was and also how strong my vibration was. *"Who me?"*

I was getting my *'fake humility'* on, trying to be modest and deflect any compliments while secretly eating it all up. Being part of this organization also opened up speaking opportunities. I studied under millionaire and billionaire mentors who were impressed with my desire to serve. As a result, I started speaking nationally and was amazed at how my voice was being heard.

I was beginning to own my voice.

THE EDUCATION
MASLOW HIERARCHY OF NEEDS

Psychologist Abraham Maslow theorized the five-tier model of human needs in 1943. He proposed that people are motivated to achieve specific needs, and once the tier is fulfilled, strive to achieve the next level until self-actualization results.

The five tiers are categorized as follows:

- ✓ **Physiological needs,** such as food and water
- ✓ **Safety needs**, such as security

- ✓ **Belongingness,** such as intimate relationships
- ✓ **Esteem needs,** such as feeling accomplished
- ✓ **Self-actualization**, such as reaching one's fullest potential

This five-tier model is further categorized by deficiency and growth needs. Physiological, safety, belongingness and esteem are classified as deficiency needs which activate deprivation when these needs are unmet. For instance, it is said the love of money is the root of all evil. However, lack of money, which falls in the physiological needs category, seems to further exacerbate the problem and we become destitute. We are not ready to go to the next level if our needs at that current level are deficient.

The top level is the growth needs to which it stems from a desire to grow and to become. When one reaches their highest potential to become who they are called to be, this is called self-actualization. It is important to note that the more our motivation decreases in the lower level tiers, the higher the probability that we regress and become stuck. The more our motivation increases in the top tier, the higher the likelihood that we have arrived at our optimal level of greatness.

Powerful person, I will switch up and give you a powerful challenge. My challenge for you is, *what is your hierarchy of needs for owning your voice?* What are your primary, intermediate and top level needs to ultimately speak your voice? This is an exercise for you to complete. Create a triangle and draw three lines inside of the triangle. Then map out what are the first level needs are that have to be met to go to the next level until you self-actualize.

For instance, my basic needs were acceptance and positive regard. My next level was affirmation and my niche, or expertise. My top tier level for self-actualization is speaking my voice which satisfies my purpose.

What's your hierarchy of needs?

THE CONVERSATION
LIFE LESSONS

Berny was my mentor. He was more like a dad. I called him my White Daddy. I remembered meeting him in California at a conference where he offered 30-minute coaching sessions for participants. We talked for about 1.5 hours because he asked me how he could support me, and I started to cry.

He said, "Aw baby, what's wrong?" "I wish I could put you on my knee and hug you and wipe your tears." I took this as a daddy-daughter moment because Berny's heart was golden. He only wishes to help business owners and entrepreneurs shine and soar in their purpose. I cried because I was having a *Cinderella moment*. I was in one of the richest counties in California, at a conference with one of the top millionaires mentoring me, who took time and interest in hearing what I had to say, and encouraging me, saying, *"There's something special about you, you're going to be the next Lisa Nichols."*

I continued crying.

Further, he said, "I am going to take you under my wing, and I'm going to help you." I still cried.

He said, "Aw, honey, what's wrong? What're the tears for?" I said, "You know, I feel like *Cinderella*. I know how to present myself, and I know how to attract people to me. I'm just waiting for the clock to strike 12 and for all of this to disappear. I know what I'm going back to when all of this is over. These are mini vacations and definitely escapes to get away from my real life."

He said, "You know what? *You can change it*. I am going to help you. I'm going to help you and demonstrate how to change it." This man was going to show me how to own my voice and claim my power.

Incredibly, that same conference that I was an attendee in California would be the same conference I would speak on stage five months later in Philadelphia. They came to Philly and afforded me an opportunity to own my voice on stage. *I couldn't believe it!* Only five months before, I was in the audience looking around wondering how I got there; now I was speaking my voice on that same stage, claiming my power.

Now, I own my voice.

THE REVELATION

TIPS AND RECOMMENDATIONS

When it comes to your journey in owning your voice and claiming your power:

SPEAK YOUR VOICE

- ✓ **Speak up by speaking your voice.** You do not know who is watching you or who is listening to what you have to say.

- ✓ **Challenge yourself beyond your comfort zone.** At the end of your comfort zone is where your success begins. Challenging yourself to network, join support groups, to speak and to serve more all play a part in building your skills and your character. It creates the confidence you need to own your voice.

- ✓ **Build your momentum.** The more you connect with others, utilizing other ways to get your voice out there, the more traction you build in claiming your power and owning your voice.

- ✓ **Think and expect the best.** Do not let your brain help you in playing small by keeping yourself out of the game called life. Instead, think and expect the best in everything you do. You will be surprised at the synergy it creates and the opportunities it summons all at the goal of owning your voice.

- ✓ **Connect with like-minded individuals to further support you in your endeavors.** It does make a world of difference to stay plugged in with others striving for similar dreams and goals.

This has been a long time coming for you, and now is the time for you to own your voice.

SELF REFLECTION EXERCISE

To **OWN** Your Voice, get into a quiet space, and give yourself 15-30 minutes to do this exercise. Reflect, free associate, and write down your first thoughts that come to mind when answering the questions below without questioning or altering your answers.

List 3 opportunities you will create for yourself to start owning your voice.

_____
_____
_____

What three networking events will you commit to attending to own your voice?

_____
_____
_____

What is it that you want to talk about if given the opportunity to speak on a topic? Why that topic?

_____
_____
_____

What are the takeaways that you have learned about yourself with regards to owning your voice?

_____
_____

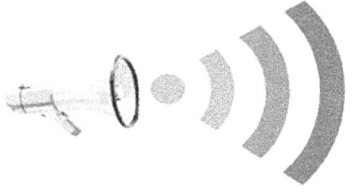

INTERLUDE #4
SARAH, ME TOO

I started as a businesswoman at a non profit organization. The owner and I had really hit it off and began our work together. I realized I loved power and I was profoundly attracted to him. Alas, a relationship ensued. I knew he was married, but I just couldn't shake him off. What left a bad taste in my mouth with him was the fact that he used his position of authority and influence over me and others to get what he wanted. I decided to break the relationship off, and suddenly he started stalking me, calling me, having my home surveillance. He wouldn't stop! He harassed me as in a threating way, as if I were ever to tell anyone of our relationship something could happen. I would be blackballed in my field. He also made it seem as if I didn't have the authority or the right to leave him as if he would tell me when he was ready to leave me or when he was done with me. This was really hard, and I cannot believe I had put myself in that situation. He didn't want to let me go, although I knew he was messing around with others at the office. I had to resign from working there because of the owner's offensive manner in how he handled one of the staff members. It was the best decision I made to finally escape from him and from that entire situation.

Sarah Renee Langley

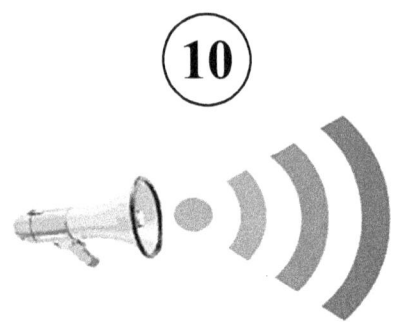

BE YOUR VOICE

YOU AND YOUR VOICE BECOMES ONE

"Not everyone will understand your journey. That's okay. You're here to live your life, not to make everyone understand."

--Bansky

SPEAK YOUR VOICE

MY NARRATIVE

What are the tears for, honey? Berny asked while I sniffled and snotted. "I feel like Cinderella.... I know what I'm going back to when all of this is over. These are mini vacations and definitely escapes to get away from my real life."

He said, "You know what? You can change it. I am going to help you. I'm going to help you and demonstrate how to change it."

Just like that, I was on stages. I was even invited to speak on stage in India! India! International bound! Merely setting the intention and having unwavering faith no matter how it looked *was vital.* It was all based on what I believed and what I was exposed to. I was in my element and in a great supportive environment to help me become one with my voice. I have a new identity and a new voice. *This was a long time coming.*

Until, April of 2016.

At the conference, I met this high powered, world-renowned businessman known for women's apparel. He was so amazed by my speech that he wanted to take a picture with me. *I was honored.*

"Wow! Do you want to take a picture with me? Absolutely sir." We found someone to take the picture. I had this beautiful flowy cream colored, long, ruffled, ballerina-type skirt, so no one could really see past the front of the skirt. When we posed for the picture, this man had the nerve to put his hand on my behind,

and no one was able to notice. I couldn't believe it. I was in shock. *"Really? How dare you think this is okay?"* I didn't know how to react because he was this prominent world- renowned businessman. For him to put his hand on my behind, smile and think that it was okay triggered my male persona once again, to claim back my power. Another participant came to us and said, *"Oh, you were amazing. Can I take a picture of the two of you?"* He said, *"Oh absolutely!"* grinning from ear to ear as he looked at me. And what do you know? *He did the same thing again!*

Now, why did I allow it a second time? I was still in shock. I still couldn't believe he thought it was okay. I started to analyze this: *"What makes you feel this is okay? What makes you think I welcome this or what sign did I give you to think it was okay to put your hand on my butt? What's so attractive about my butt to these men?"*

I did not know what to think or what to say. But like many of us do, I let it go and shrugged it off.

He's just being a man.

It's interesting. You start coming to know who you are, your confidence rising, your clarity is evident, your courage is impressive, your strength is unmistakable, and then the *unthinkable happens.* Someone attempts to mute your voice and take your power by usurping their authority and influence by putting their hand on your behind, and smile and think it is okay. So much for my male persona coming out to beat him up! I felt that I couldn't expose that side of myself in that setting. I couldn't let Renee come out. *So Sarah had* to remain and mute our voices.

What would you have done in this situation? Have you ever experienced something similar?

Recently, women and men have courageously owned their voices and claimed their power by speaking their voices and calling foul on media and entertainment moguls on sexual misconduct and sexual assault. It was like a domino effect starting from one of the top producers in the entertainment industry to well--beloved actors that you would have never thought sexually assaulted someone.

Here's the thing. There is nothing new about sexual assault, harassment, or misconduct. There are plenty of stories out there, known and unknown. Many suffer in silence because their perpetrator was an unknown. How to get their stories out there and help them be their voices?

Where's Tarana Burke when you need her?

THE EDUCATION
STRESS MANAGEMENT

According to the National Health Interview Survey, about 75% of the general population experience some form of stress every two weeks. Approximately 1 million Americans are absent from work due to a stress-related disorder. More Americans are utilizing professional health services to help manage stress- related issues. Ninety percent of visits to the doctor are for stress-related complaints, with stress being the 6th leading cause of death. Job stress costs the U.S. industry 300 billion dollars annually due to low productivity, absenteeism employee turnover, and more recently, caregiving for disabled parents.

What is stress? Stress is physical, mental, emotional, or behavioral responses we give towards a demand or situation. We respond the same regardless of the stressor. It's like an internal alarm system.

Our sympathetic nervous system is designed to respond in a flight, fight or freeze mode. Our responses to stress affects every part of our bodily system; blood vessels, immune system, digestive system, sensory organs, and brain, just to meet the demand or the *perceived* danger. Stress can result from our perception or thought about the event. An example is preparing for my book release party. If this book isn't ready in time for the party, I would be nervous or anxious because of my perceptions of what others would think of me. And that sucks.

There are 3 types of stress.

Acute stress, or short-term stress, is experienced in response to an immediate perceived threat, either physical, emotional or psychological. The perceived threat can be real or imagined; it's the *perception* of danger that triggers the response. An example is a near missed car accident, with the oncoming car as the threat, and your response is getting out of the way. Common emotional symptoms are irritability, anxiety, and depression. Muscular problems are back pain and headaches. Stomach/ bowel problems are heartburn, or diarrhea, and elevation of blood pressure, heart palpitations, and sweaty hands, based on the chemicals released in your system to react to the perceived threat or danger.

Episodic stress occurs when life's situations get the best of us. One example is when you believed you deserved a raise or promotion and you didn't get it. Another example is when life spins out of control with one disaster after another, such as an illness, divorce, and loss of employment within a short time span.

Chronic Stress, also known as long-term stress, is the type of stress that grinds away at you over long periods of time or by past experiences. Examples include poverty, dysfunctional families, or feeling trapped in an unhappy marriage or in a job. We aren't aware of chronic stress at times because it's familiar, it's comfortable, and we're used to it. However, chronic stress can lead to death through suicide, violence, heart attack, stroke, or disease.

When there is a perceived threat, one will respond with a **Flight/Fight or Freeze Reaction.** Flight or fight or freeze reactions are when one either runs or avoids the situation, remains and fights in the situation, or freezes and doesn't move in the situation.

WARNING: I get techy so that you can fully understand the intricate details of how the flight/fight/freeze reactions work.

Flight/Fight/Freeze reactions occur when a trigger is confirmed as a threat by the parts of the limbic system, the brain's alarm center. The limbic system directs the sympathetic nervous system (SNS) to alert the body. The SNS stimulates the adrenal medulla, located near the kidneys, to release the adrenaline-like compounds, epinephrine, and norepinephrine, into the bloodstream. The limbic system also tells the hypothalamus, the control center of the brain, to signal the tiny pituitary gland near the brainstem to create other chemical signals to help further activate the body. As a result of action on the pituitary, the adrenal cortex releases cortisol, an important stress hormone. The release of these chemicals causes changes in the body's ability to respond to threats in the fight, flight, or freeze modes such as increased energy, heart rate, and blood sugar or increased arousal and pain relief.

Which mode do you typically operate in, flight, fight, or freeze? Why is that?

How do you cope with stress? It's not the event that determines the outcome but how you *respond* to it. Know that you can't control or manipulate the event at times, so learn how to manage your reactions and feelings and thoughts about the event. One strategy is taking 20 minutes to meditate, relax, and unplug. Another coping strategy is to accept the things that you can't change. Plan ahead with things that you can to lessen the stress. You can also change your responses by thinking more positively and set the intention to come out on top with owning your voice.

Lastly, know the difference between effective and ineffective coping strategies. Instead of being overly committed and needing to prove yourself, focus on what you can manage, one thing at a time, plan ahead, and perform self-care---it makes a world of difference. Additionally, reprioritize your life, accept the things you cannot change, accept your assets and your shortcomings, and stop and take breaths. Inhale and exhale deep breaths so that you can reposition and merely say SATORI.

Powerful person, let me ask you these powerful questions: *Do you have any stressors in your life that you need to let go? How might you be contributing to the stress? What do you commit to in order to change your situation so that you are no longer stressed out?*

THE CONVERSATION
LIFE LESSONS

Anita Hill. Paula Jones. Monica Lewinsky. These are notable names of the 1990s. These women accused men who held the highest positions in the land for sexual harassment and misconduct.

Attorney Anita Hill, then 35 years old in 1991, testified before the U.S. Senate Judiciary Committee to bring up sexual harassment allegations against then-Supreme Court Justice Nominee, Clarence Thomas. I was 14 at the time and remember watching the televised court proceedings. I did not understand all that was going on, but isn't it something that over 25 years later, we are still bringing up sexual assault, harassment and misconduct allegations? What have we not learned from the Hill/

Thomas Trial that causes us to repeat history in such a progressive time of the 21st century?

I can only imagine what Ms. Hill thought when she said, "You know what? I am going to say something." I can only imagine that she calculated and counted the costs; the shame, ridicule, embarrassment, humiliation, ostracism and judgment, merely for her believing that it was not okay to sexually harass her. The way she and the case were handled during the All Male Senate Judiciary Committee hearings spoke volumes of the kind of society we lived in back then, and unfortunately even now. Hill is an icon for courageously speaking her voice against the injustices of sexual harassment, even when it was at the expense of her job as a professor at the University of Oklahoma, at the cost of ridicule, and at the expense of no longer having privacy.

As history shows, Thomas became court justice, and we seemed to have moved on. It is astonishing that we are having this conversation, ironically around the same time that Anita Hill testified. In October 2017, movie producer, Harvey Weinstein was accused of raping 3 women and sexually harassing dozens of others, which resulted in what the media called the *Weinstein Effect*. Since then, over 71 high profiled men either resigned or was fired from their positions, with 28 more having faced suspensions. Before 2017, society notoriously misplaced blame on victims instead of on the perpetrators. Now, society is reacting, and these top moguls are being fired. There are accusations, but no one has yet to be officially charged with the recent allegations.

SPEAK YOUR VOICE

What's up with being reactive instead of proactive?

Now, don't get me wrong, for those who have admitted their shortcomings, perhaps it was well deserved for them losing their jobs. However, it seems like reaction begets reaction. The story of the lawmaker in Kentucky who took his own life over the accusation that was made against him begs the question: *"How should we properly handle this situation?"*

Who are the winners? The women and men who were sexually assaulted or harassed suffered in silence for far too long. Yet, they are questioned on what took them so long to report. The overarching theme has been fear of retaliation and being blackballed. The men accused of these crimes weren't charged yet but have fallen from grace, humiliated, and shamed. Some vehemently denied any wrongdoing, like news commentator Tavis Smiley, and are fighting to clear their names from this ever-growing list. What is unfortunate is that *it is nothing new*. Abuse of power, the lust of control, and desire to subjugate has been in the world's DNA for centuries. I dare say the companies and organizations that the men worked knew about their incorrigible indiscretions and yet, did nothing until the *shit hit the fan.*

IJS.

Presumably, these big corps swiftly took action by firing or suspending the accused, perhaps to keep their endorsements intact and to keep their doors open.

Once you're taken to Twitter, it's over for you!

Right, Tony?

Nevertheless, I am proud of the women and men who owned their voices by speaking out. I wish I did. This is my way to speak my voice to the man who groped me. It is not okay to assault, rape, harass, touch....wait, is there a *difference between rape and sexual assault?* This is the problem we have as a society with lack of clarity on what rape or any unwanted sexual advances mean. According to an article in Slate, penal codes in the U.S. court system classifies sexual assault and rape differently per state. For instance, Pennsylvania, the state I am from, says in statute books that rape requires using of threat or force, but sexual assault refers to any sexual act without consent. Additionally, sexual assault didn't become a legal term until the 1960s, with any form of sex crimes rarely prosecuted. Even by this definition, it is still unclear to me as to *why it is unclear!*

This shows that dialogue is needed to remove the guesswork, and frankly, the justifications and ways out of holding perpetrators to the highest form of accountability and responsibility for their actions. Additionally, companies and organizations need to create better rules and guidelines on the integrity and character of their employees who represent them. Most importantly, those who have experienced deplorable acts of rape and harassment must also speak their voices to become one with their voice. That is the way of getting your power back, by merely speaking your voice, regardless and despite of all that comes with the price of speaking it. Think of how many you are saving and protecting as a result of you speaking your voice.

SPEAK YOUR VOICE

Look at the greater picture at large.

Anita Hill not only represented her voice, but she represented our voices. The Washington Post reported that Ms. Hill chairs the Commission on Sexual Harassment and Advancing Equality in the Workplace. Its mission is to "tackle the broad culture of abuse and power disparity... creating a comprehensive strategy to address the complex and interrelated causes of the problems of parity and power."

We will see how it goes.

Bottom line, be one with your voice by sharing your story, your message, and truth. Accept that you went through what you have gone through for a reason, and it is to help someone go from victims to victors. The whole world is waiting and watching for you to speak your voice. What better time to start than now, showing all of us your true and authentic self, born and design to be your voice and help give permission for others to be their voices, too.

Be Your Voice.

THE REVELATION
TIPS AND RECOMMENDATIONS

Know that you are here on purpose. It is not by happenstance that you are here. You are *Not* a mistake. The question is, are you living on purpose? Do you know what your purpose is? Did I ask you earlier if you even know who you are? One thing is sure, you are a representative of your own voice. Your unique story is for someone else to take notes on how to overcome and triumph over similar situations and circumstances. To reframe your mindset and become one with your voice, do the following:

- ✓ Accept that we learn how to stand and become whole by a healthy balance of life's challenges and beautiful outcomes. Life challenges to show us what we are made of. When we buck against and refuse to accept this, we repeat the challenges until we do concede. Know this, every day may not be a great day but every day is a learning day. You do not fail. You either win or you learn. What are you learning on your journey of being your voice?

- ✓ There is a benefit in sharing with others your story. You message matters and can make a world of difference in the lives that you touch, even if you are not speaking. The story of my mom is an excellent example for this point.

- ✓ You are your Why. What you have been through puts you in position to be vulnerable, tangible, understanding, relatable, and available to others who have experienced similar problems. Who is to say by being your voice, it helps set the captives, who might have lost their way, free?

- ✓ Add more value to your voice. Study those who share similar circumstances, those you admire, and what they have done to, ultimately, be their voices as a beacon of

SPEAK YOUR VOICE

light for others

- ✓ Once again, accept that it is your duty and obligation to speak voice to help free lives, transform lives, touch lives, and shift lives into their rightful places in this world.

It starts with you being your voice to ultimately speak your voice.

Sarah Renee Langley

SELF REFLECTION EXERCISE

To **BE** your voice, get into a quiet space, and give yourself 15-30 minutes to do this exercise. Reflect, free associate, and write down your first thoughts that come to mind when answering the questions below without questioning or altering your answers.

What is one thing you will commit to in order to become one with your voice? How will you support your efforts and how will you celebrate your efforts?

_____
_____
_____

How will you maintain self-care throughout this process of speaking your voice?

_____
_____
_____

What causes are you passionate to support and why?

_____
_____
_____

What is one change, good, bad, or indifferent, that you have noticed about yourself since reading this book? How do you feel about it?

_____
_____
_____

SPEAK YOUR VOICE

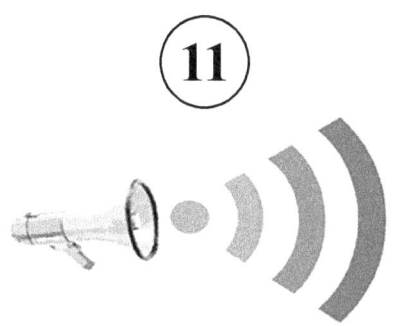

GIVE YOUR VOICE
GIVE BACK

"From what we get, we can make a living; what we give, however, make a life."

– Winston Churchill.

Sarah Renee Langley
MY NARRATIVE

He groped me! While taking a picture! Twice! He grabbed the same area! The same area that the male doctor pointed to over 10 years before. Where is human dignity and respect? What makes folks think it's okay to violate others and entirely discount their rights? And why didn't I speak up?

Well, I did. Somewhat.

Toward the end of the conference was a soiree and everyone was decked out and snazzy. In the ballroom, I ran into the guy who groped me earlier, and wouldn't you know, someone asked to take a picture of us! I cannot make this up! As he prepared to get ready to grab my behind again, I literally grabbed his hand and placed it exactly where it was supposed to go which was around my waist. I grew tired of his attempts, and my voice within conveyed through my reaction that he was not to touch me ever again. I would direct where his hands go for any future photo ops.

He didn't say anything. And he didn't take any more pics with me, except a group usie with another woman. I made sure I took my power right back before the night ended. *How would you have handled the situation?* I can only image who else had to experience that ordeal since or before then.

It is important to speak our voice so that others can speak theirs. However, there are others who do not have a voice to speak. *You could be one of them.* How do you get your message and story out?

SPEAK YOUR VOICE

Simple. By giving your voice however you can.

My dad brought us up to think that we would be famous. As a singer and guitarist, my dad tried to make my brothers and me the next Jackson 5 or something like that. My brothers would be so jealous of me because I was the lead singer all the time. I was the only girl, so it was more like Gladys Knight and the Pips.

Around Christmas time, me and one of my brothers, Andre, would sing to seniors in nursing homes. To see these seniors light up with smiles on their faces as we gave our voices was priceless. When you give your voice to those who do not have one, it is freeing and liberating. What's even more exhilarating for me is to give my voice to the very one who had given me a voice since day one. And that is my beloved mother, Mary.

My mom had such a heart of advocacy for the less fortunate and underprivileged. She also had such an amazing, magnetic, electrifying smile that drew everyone to her. She was once a model for the Sears department store. Elegant, graceful, and beautiful, my 5-foot 2-inch little lady has been a friendly, kind, and sweet woman. Mom is a Libra, and she definitely was all about fairness and justice; if she felt it was unfair, Mom would muster up the courage to give her voice about it. Mom was shy and quiet, but was kicking down doors in the name of activism during the 70s, challenging Philly's vending and housing ordinances, as so my Dad puts it. The famous Street Brothers in Philadelphia spoke out for black communities against unfairness and injustice for the underprivileged.

And my dad would say, *"You know what? I don't know why she's out there, going out there running around with those Street Boys! If she goes to jail, I am still going to work. I am not going to bail her out."* That statement also goes for his kids, too.

It was a great thing that none of us put his rule to the test.

I had watched Mom give her voice in the name of justice 30 of my 41 years. If any of the family members spoke out against another, she stood by that family member. If that same family member now joins the numbers and speaks out against the next family member, Mom would then stand by that family member. Mom respected and protected us all the same. None of us ever went against Mom. We would have lost!

My Mom gave her voice to the voiceless until she no longer could use hers. Alzheimer's Disease robbed her of her voice. All she does now is hum, but in that hum, I know what she is saying because I'm her daughter, I'm her child.

As I initially struggled to accept Mom's fate, my pastor said that God built me in such a way that I was going to be her voice. I thought that was a tall order. At that time I was in search of my own voice. I was about to take on the most difficult and most rewarding responsibility I ever had: holding a woman in my hands who had once held me in hers.

I share this with you because I want you to understand the difference between being your voice and being someone else's voice. You have to count the cost of giving your voice and the holistic preparation it warrants to effectively and efficiently give it. Do not get lost in the sauce of giving your voice and depleting yours in the name of others.

Mom would tell me that without telling me when I went to a business mastermind near San Diego, California.

THE EDUCATION

MOTIVATION

What is your motivation? What motivates you? What is motivation? Webster Merriam Dictionary defines motivation *as the desire or willingness of someone to do something, or the reason one has for acting or behaving a particular way.* At times, we need to think about our motivators when we are executing our goals and desires. In the coaching world, we call it our why. What is your why? Is it compelling enough to take action on your goals, or it doesn't move you at all? That is when you need to reconsider what is your real motivator and the value you place on it.

Psychologist, Frederick Herzberg, theorized the two- factor theory of motivation, which discusses how particular factors cause job satisfaction and other specific factors create dissatisfaction in the workplace. Herzberg conducted his study involving blue and white collar workers, and he analyzed how job satisfaction with relation to what one does was equivalent to satisfaction when tied to achievement, status and personal worth. On the contrary, dissatisfaction stemmed from unfavorable assessments to company policies, supervision, and pay. A presentation by at the RSA-Royal Society for the Encouragement of Arts, Manufactures, and Commerce supplements Herzberg argument in that motivators to better performance isn't money when the work requires complex thinking. Motivators to better performance and satisfaction are autonomy, mastery, and purpose. Otherwise, performance increased when rewarded with money for mechanical skills.

Herzberg concluded that the nature of the work increases satisfaction and better job environment decreases dissatisfaction. Furthermore, Herzberg's two-factor theory differentiates between motivators like being challenged at work, recognition for employee's contribution to the vision of the company, and autonomy, to what is called Hygiene or maintenance factors, like job security and salary. It is important to point out that motivation is needed to inspire higher performance.

In properly giving your voice, discovering the power of purpose as a motivating factor is very rewarding. You will feel like you made a difference in someone's life simply because you gave your voice to those who do not have one. Discover your why, what motivates you to give your voice so that you show others how to do the same thing.

THE CONVERSATION

LIFE LESSONS

I was attending a weekend mastermind retreat in California. It was incredible driving along the highways and seeing the breathtaking scenery. Beautiful mountain views and flat desert lands were to die for. I never noticed any mountains in Philly! It was a treat that's for sure. We met with our mastermind hosts as they greeted the participants at this gorgeous hotel that had a fantastic courtyard and garden. I am very visual and was stimulated by the surroundings. I enjoyed every moment in this *Fairytaleland* and was ready to turn this into *Realityville* for myself.

We all shared our expectations of this retreat and what we were willing to do to grow ourselves and our businesses. We also talked about the barriers we faced and how these barriers were holding us back. I participated in an Inipi ceremony. An Inipi ceremony is a purification process that prepares individuals for some form of divine intervention as a common Native American practice. Inipi is a term that means '*to live again,*' helping us get into a place of humility and experience a spiritual rebirth. As we shared our most intimate thoughts surrounding our barriers and our desires, I thought about my mother and how drained I was in caring for her. I never admitted this because I did not want Mom to feel as if she was a burden on me.

This purification process helped me to realize how connected Mom and I were and with that I was able to hear her tell me something while I was in this tent, sweating the toxins away. I know this may sound deep or creepy, but it was as if Mom was spiritually talking to me from Pennsylvania while I was somewhere in California. I never wanted to admit to her how I felt for risk she would die hearing my concern. I am going to share with you what *my Mom said to me in my spirit:*

"My dear child, I love you, but you have a life. I lived my life; don't you dare give your life to me for me to live because you need your life to live. You have a purpose and a calling on your life, and you must fulfill it. I already lived my life. I did everything I wanted to do. I was a mother, and I was a wife, and I took joy in raising all of you. I took joy in being a friend; I took joy in being a wife. I went to school. I got my degree. I was able to take care of people all of my life; that is the joy that I had. So if I were to end right now, I'm satisfied, but don't you dare give your life to me for me to live because you need your life to live for you. Others are waiting for you to help them to live, too."

Floodgates of tears again.

Did Mom just make you cry, too? Her powerful message hit me so hard back then as it does now while writing this book. That was the moment I understood about giving my voice. My mommy told me to give my voice without it being to my detriment. That message set me free from all other issues I harbored, especially the problems of protecting myself from being raped, again. I realized the more I focused on being taken advantage of, the more I put myself in harm's way of it happening. Why?

Because *you get what you think.*

I realized I had to stop thinking up those treacherous people who wanted to diminish my value and start thinking up those beautiful people who wanted to add to my value. And since then, those lovely people showed up in my life because I made room in my heart and mind for them.

Let it go.

How is holding on to that person, place or thing serving you? How is it showing up in your life? How does it add value? You have to determine what helps you and what depletes you. What depletes you needs to be cut off. What adds to you has to be multiplied. Remember, nothing changes unless you change. It is time for you to be in the position to give your voice and help others to live.

Mom gave her voice to me for me to give my voice to you. Mom is not able-bodied, yet she gives her voice to the masses all over the world based on our love for one another during our caregiving journey. I wouldn't change one bit of this process. It played a part in creating this book for you and others who are in need of unmuting their voices, being heard, and getting their power back.

Powerful person, here is your powerful question. *What are you doing?* What are you doing with your gifts, talents, skills and time? Stop looking at what you don't have and start looking at what you do have. Stop wondering about what if it doesn't work and start looking at what if it does work. Stop looking at your quirks and hang-ups and start looking at what you do possess. You are equipped with everything you need to win in life. Activate it so that you can exercise and master the art of giving your voice.

Another good place to practice giving your voice is by networking. One key to success is relationship building. Collaborate and create strategic partnerships and alliances not solely for what you can get but for how you can add. Become an asset of great value to this world. You do have to take action to activate and get going in your life. Invest in yourself through strengthening your voice through counseling, coaching or consulting services to raise your worth and value for the people you were born and design to serve. I always tell my clients, "Do not despise your small beginnings and don't curse the darkness of your trials and tribulations." Just be a light in your dark times so that others who are following you have a lighted path at the end of their tunnel. Be that light as an example to others that they let their light shine, too. By giving your voice to help others, it positions you to be at the right place at the right time for the right opportunity to come your way for your ultimate success and happiness. Whatever your hearts' desire, set the intention and keep it in view because you are exercising the principle of sowing and reaping.

My mom sowed love, happiness, peace, and time into my brothers and me. She has been an excellent investor. Mom is now reaping the benefits of what she has sown years before. Despite Mom having Alzheimer's Disease, she is enjoying the trip to Disneyland, spa days, her home with a balcony overlooking the city skyline, a beautiful courtyard filled with greenery, and a loving and supportive husband, daughter and caregivers by her side.

What are you sowing? For what you sow that you shall reap. Check your seeds before you place them in the ground, and make sure its good soil that you can till to expect a significant harvest in due season.

Lastly, learn to give your voice during the most difficult of times. That accelerates your growth and character. Do not succumb to what life throws at you, but it's about taking advantage of it, to learn from it, to do something different and get different results. Take notes of your life lessons during your process so that you can actively give your voice to others about what you have learned. You are giving your voice to the voiceless, setting the example for those with voices, and creating a legacy through your contribution for those who don't yet have a voice. Get in formation to give your voice so that others may apply your life lessons and your message.

Give your voice.

THE REVELATION
TIPS AND RECOMMENDATIONS

- ✓ Powerful person, respectfully, get out of your own way for others to get into position. Let go of whatever it is that's occupying space in your life that drains and depletes you. Accept that it doesn't serve you for the bigger picture and that there are plenty in line waiting for you to give your voice.

- ✓ Start becoming the best version of yourself. Grow in skill, knowledge, and experience to add significant value to your life and in others.

- ✓ Network and collaborate with others, particularly those who are running faster than you, meaning those who you can glean from. It opens doors for new opportunities and fresh new perspective on life when connecting with others.

- ✓ Put yourself in a position to give your voice, whether through blogging, podcasting, or through talks. If public speaking scares you, find opportunities to speak and do it scared! Meetup.com is something that can help you create your own mini event or group for people to come to and hear your message of hope and promise taken from your playbook of life lessons.

- ✓ Think of other avenues to give your voice. Remember, you will significantly reap what you have sown in the lives you touch. Set the intention to give your voice now.

SPEAK YOUR VOICE
SELF REFLECTION EXERCISE

To **GIVE** Your Voice, get into a quiet space, and give yourself 15-30 minutes to do this exercise. Reflect, free associate, and write down your first thoughts that come to mind when answering the questions below without questioning or altering your answers.

List all of the ways you presently give your voice.

_____
_____
_____

List three ways you will now give your voice differently.

_____
_____
_____

List three things you commit to letting go that drains and depletes you in order to make room for new opportunities to come in your life.

_____
_____
_____

What is one new skill or knowledge you plan to obtain to add more value to giving your voice to others? Why that skill?

_____
_____
_____

INTERLUDE #5
SARAH, ME TOO

Early in my career, I had the opportunity to travel with my company. On one of the trips, my direct boss who was an attorney traveled with me. After the day's events and meetings were over and we were settled in for the evening, I received a call on my hotel room phone from my boss. He said that he wanted me to come over to his room to end the night with sex. I promptly told him, "No that is not appropriate," and hung up. I was so taken back by this that I made myself physically ill. I had multiple fever blisters and had to miss work. I worked up the nerve to tell the office manager. I also explained this is why I had been out and had fever blisters. She came to see me at my house the next day and told me that unfortunately, I had not been the first this had happened to and that, in fact, the company had been sued. She offered me two months severance and asked that I sign paperwork saying I would not sue. This was an awful experience and even though I knew it was wrong and I did nothing wrong, it was still challenging to tell.

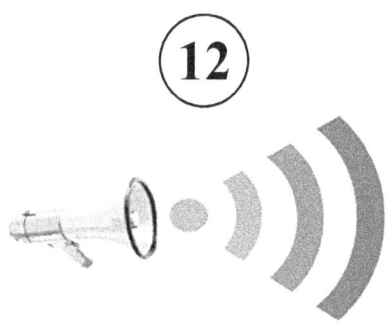

SHARE YOUR VOICE

THAT'S YOUR RESPONSIBILITY

"Life is so much better when you share it."

--Oprah Winfrey

Sarah Renee Langley

MY NARRATIVE

"*Don't you dare give your life to me for me to live because you need your life to live for you. Others are waiting for you to help them to live.*" Words from my Mom while she was in Pennsylvania and I was in California by way of our spiritual connection. I hope you read the previous chapter to know what I am talking about.

Throughout this process I have learned how to search, find, get, build, hear, love, show, own, be, and give my voice. Finally, it was time for me to share my voice because that is my responsibility. Anita Hill shared this notion in an interview, believing that she had a duty to share what she endured by Clarence Thomas as to prevent sexual harassment from happening to others. When we go through something, we need to share it for preventive measures for others.

As a counselor, I offered free services to victims' families who have lost a loved one due to violence. During the holidays, I posted free grief and loss services on Facebook for those in need. I shared my voice to help them deal with the pain and trauma and appropriately grieve.

Like me, you may have experienced significant trauma that resulted in losing your voice along the way, but understand when it comes to sexual assault, harassment or misconduct, you get your voice back by getting your power back. Rape isn't about sex but about power, dominance, and control. The way that you get your power back is to speak your voice. But know that it does not stop there.

SPEAK YOUR VOICE

Many are stuck in time because of the violations that have happened and do not know the first thing about speaking their voices.

You do. Yes, *you do.*

They need you to share your voice with them about your traumatic experiences and how you overcame them. You merely didn't go through what you had gone through just for some book deal or cameo appearance. Rather, you have gone through what you have gone through because it was purposed to happen. That may be a hard pill to swallow, believe me I know. Yet, accept that everything happens for a reason

What are you going to do about it?

After the book deal and exclusive rights to your story, after the red carpets and cameo appearances and interviews, once you go home, take off the fancy clothes, jewelry, and makeup, then you have to look at yourself in the mirror and ask these questions: *Did I really share my voice? Did I do all I was to do in sharing my voice? Did it impact a life, save a life, prevent anyone from going down the same road I was on? Did I share my voice?*

There are unsung sheroes and heroes out there who haven't had the luxury of sharing their stories to the media because their perpetrators were unknowns. That doesn't make their stories any less relevant just because we go from one hot topic to the next hot topic. At the time of writing this book, the new movement was created by teen aged children, *marching for their lives*, to protect themselves against gun violence in the schools. The Speak Your Voice initiative is more than a 1st quarter trend. It is a lifestyle to learning how to indeed speak your voice.

I will share one more narrative with you in hopes to motivate, empower, and inspire you to share your voice with others.

WARNING: What I am about to share with you is something I haven't shared with anyone.

Except for those in my harem.

I didn't stutter.

I was invited to speak in India and met the most amazing people from all over the world! One hundred and eight countries were represented in this powerful women's forum and it was utterly incredible. Dining with princesses and Your Royal Highnesses and them bearing gifts of gratitude and friendship was mind-blowing. *I was no longer Cinderella.* The clock struck 12 and nothing happened. My dreams turned into realities.

After India, I went to another conference to keep the momentum going with more networking and gaining prospects. On my way to one of the workshops, this gentleman stopped me and asked which workshop I decided to attend. I told him, and he asked me to follow him instead. He wanted to talk about my business. The gentleman expressed how impressed he was with my appearance and said I was one of the most powerful women he has ever met, next to one other person who was disabled. He wanted to know more about me.

SPEAK YOUR VOICE

The gentleman proclaimed to be a self-made millionaire and businessman, and he attended to me the entire weekend I was at the conference. We soon began developing a budding relationship. A *secret one.*

Initially, as most relationships start out, our relationship was in the honeymoon phase, full of laughter, drinks, dinner, conversations, and sex. It was an outstanding secret love affair. No one pegged us. I would travel to meet him, and I would soak up his knowledge and wisdom. From heated debates to convos that were total turn-ons, we seemed to have been going in the right direction with our relationship. No commitment, no strings attached. Neither one of us were looking for a long-term relationship. If something developed, we were allowing things to happen naturally.

Yet, something didn't feel right.

I am very perceptive and discerning. I heard in my spirit,

"*If you continue to be with him, he's going to kill you.*"

Wowzers. Where did that come from? Something I ate? No, it was something that stayed in the back of my mind, but also something I was willing to test. Why? Because I started to lust after his power.

Our honeymoon period was winding down. We argued more over a couple of things. One primary source of contention was my harem. Yes, I had a harem. No, it really wasn't a harem by definition, but that is what all the men that were part of my dating circle called it. I was dating four men at once. Don't worry, they all knew about the other. I hated liars and was not about to lie to any of them, so I informed each one of them that I was dating at least three others. *Men do it! Why can't women?* I told all of them the rules of engagement, and while they all hated it, they all complied. This particular one, the millionaire, didn't like the competition and felt like the other three were not in his league. He always wanted me to let them go. However, in fairness, I did not ask him to let go of whomever he dated. I decided to keep my boy toys. He said, "As long as you know when to put your toys away when you are with me."

Ok, that's fair.

The 2nd source of contention was me saying no to him. He hated the word no. He believed that everyone was subjected to his demands and to do what he tells them to do, including me. You know me enough to know by now that neither Renee nor Sarah was bowing down to him.

That is when shit hit the fan again.

Our relationship became tumultuous, full of insults, demands, and broken promises. It became a game of who gets who first. It was becoming dangerous. He started introducing S & M conversations, which for the record, I never complied, and that kindled his anger the more. Apparently, he wasn't dating anyone else while we were seeing each other.

SPEAK YOUR VOICE

"I don't understand how I can get any woman I want. I am prestigious, an overall good looking guy, and politician. I can get pussy any time I want, and I can get my dick sucked. But with you I have to ask for it and not get it?! And I ask myself why I am fucking with her holding out for her, not seeing anybody else, and I keep hearing no!"

It should be evident that I was playing the field and being the dominant man among these men girls! Not to insult any of them. This was the script we all decided to follow. No one chose to change it. Maybe it was unusual for all of us to see who could make me change my mind and become a one-man woman. Perhaps it was a sexy concept to be involved in our tightly knit harem. I know it triggered my automatic thoughts:

"None of you are going to dominate me. None of you are going to take advantage of me. I will take advantage of you first and be ok with it."

How did this old narrative become alive all over again?

I became so engrossed in him as to how he had a cult following of hundreds of thousands concerning his business services. I found it fascinating how he impacted and mobilized people to take action to work with him and for him. It was remarkable. *I wanted that*. I wanted his type of power. And at that moment, *I started losing myself again*. He knew that was my weakness, and he took total advantage of my desire for power and control. "Come on over so I can help you with your business. I will show you how to dominate your market."

Anita Hill was asked why she continued working for Clarence Thomas after being sexually harassed. She shared that she thought more about her professional advancement as opposed to anything else. I only focused on dominating the coaching and speaking world at all costs. I didn't count the costs. I became prideful, thinking that I could handle this guys' dark world, but he was winning. His goal was to now *"subjugate me."* "I am going to own you. You will submit to me," he would tell me. I would say to myself, *over my dead body*. All the while, I was mentally subjugated, and I didn't know. He had a mental hold on me that I believed I couldn't break because of the value I placed on having power over my dignity and self-worth. I started doing things he wanted me to do. From submission chairs to going to swinging clubs and finding vulnerable victims

to tag team and subjugate them, even if it resulted in injurious behavior. I entertained any idea he suggested.

What in the world did I get myself into? How do I get out of it? Why don't I want to get out of it?

He began mentally and emotionally punishing me. He said, "The men you are dating are weak. I am pure Alpha male. In fact, I am the Alpha of all Alphas. I am dominating you on behalf of all the men you subjugate. I am doing to you what you do to them. You need to stay in your place. I want to own you because that is what women should be. *Owned.*"

In mental anguish, I cried and told the other three men I dated about this experience. They all said I needed to let him go, and if

I decided otherwise, to be very careful. I couldn't tell anyone else about this. Why?

My image. My perfect mask. I am supposed to be a Christian, innocent, quiet, ambitious, hardworking young lady who takes care of her parents. Who could I *share my voice with without getting judged?*

Defense mechanisms were at its highest, and pride settled. *"I'm not getting got. I will get him first. Lord, I am so far gone, and I don't want to lose myself again. I don't want this to be tragic. But if he continues to push, it's going to be him or me."*

I am in full disclosure with you because you or someone you know is experiencing this right now. It is my responsibility to share my voice with you. Therefore, I am giving you a way out so that at least you are presented with a choice to stay in or stay out.

I swear, I hope you choose the latter.

There is a term called internalizing the oppressor. It means I behaved just like the guy who raped me over 20 years ago. I was susceptible to attracting that type of lifestyle and that type of person who desired dominance and control over me. I am being real with you because we often do not want to share our voices on matters like these, but it needs to be shared. It may save a life.

I romanticized the entire situation; his promises to go away together and have fun, dancing, becoming a power couple, sounded amazing. I focused on what he said to me while ignoring what he had done to me.

He totally beat me at this game. I was subjugated

I tried to beat him at his own game with the risk of losing my life. Literally. Not figuratively.

I almost did, when he had banged me up against the wall and started choking me.

THE EDUCATION

THE FIVE LAWS OF SUCCESS

Do you want to be successful? What is success? You are. You are success. It is not what you do, but what you become that epitomizes success. But to become success, you have to check out of your comfort zone. Powerful person, my powerful question to you is, "Why only a small percentage of people like Oprah, Bill Gates and Elon Musk are among the top elite who are filthy rich and successful?" Here's why.

My hero, Jim Rohn said it best, "It's easy to do. And it is easy not to do." It is easy to be rich and to be successful. It is just as easy not to, and that is when neglect of doing the easy things that can make you money keeps you broke busted and disgusted. With that said, let's look at ways to help you become a success in no time.

Have you heard of **The Five Laws of Stratospheric Success?** Authors Bob Burg and John David Mann have written a book called the *Go-Giver*. It is a story about a man struggling to meet his sales goals; he met someone that taught him the Five

SPEAK YOUR VOICE

Laws of Stratospheric Success by gleaning from others who have conquered the five laws. Here are the five laws of success for you to master in your life and business.

The Law of Value is knowing that your true worth is determined by how much more you give in value than what you take in payment. Raise your skills and knowledge base to be of value and to give value to others.

The Law of Compensation is knowing that your income is predicated by how many and how well you serve people. Your earnings are not based on trading hours for dollars. Instead, it is based on having an entrepreneurial and marketing mindset, not an employee mindset.

The Law of Influence is based on how much you place others' interest over your own. Zig Ziglar said *you can get everything you want in life when you help enough people get what they want in life*. Put their needs first because people can smell desperation a mile away and will not use your services if they perceive that you are making it about you more than them.

The Law of Authenticity is knowing that you being 100% real and authentic is the most valuable gift you can give to others. To be real in a currently fake world takes skill nowadays. It is refreshing when you can be authentic and demonstrate that it is ok to be you for others to follow suit.

Lastly, **The Law of Receptivity** is based on being a receiver as well as a giver. Being open to receiving can be difficult for many, like me, especially when women have innate intuitiveness to give and to nurture. Therefore, staying open to receive has to be a practice for the Law of Receptivity to take effect.

Therefore, to be in a position to share your voice, you need to apply these Five Laws of Stratospheric Success to make that much more of an impact in the lives you are called to serve.

THE CONVERSATION

LIFE LESSONS

This book was for you. You needed me to share my voice to help you share your voice so that we can help set the captives free together.

Speaking your voice is not a trend, fad or a new drama series coming out in the fall. There are unsung sheroes and heroes whose voices need to be heard, whose voices need to be spoken. I genuinely believe that if enough voices are spoken on issues of sexual assault, harassment, and misconduct, things will begin to change for the better. It starts with you sharing your voice. You have something to share that is empowering and freeing You're sharing your voice for all of us to share our voices. Sharing your voice helps to set the example as a duty to help our sisters and brothers know that they are not alone. Sharing your voice helps them to know they are not the only ones going through or have gone through the same thing. Sharing your voice helps prevent our sisters and brothers from going down the same path you and I did by telling our story.

SPEAK YOUR VOICE

Your voice matters. Your message matters.

Here is the conclusion of the millionaire who almost killed me.

The pain, disappointment, and sadness I had as a result of my relationship with the millionaire guy, or lack thereof, developed into a quiet rage and disdain for him. I wanted to be with him, and whenever he had an event, I went. I would dress up in my very best to garner his attention and stay inconspicuous with our relationship. We would hook up after events and have an amazing night together, except, that's where it was left, at night. No real acknowledgment during the day because he said he didn't want to give us away, although he would acknowledge everyone but me, so it didn't make sense. In fact, I couldn't believe I relived my college days all over again as a *booty call*! Me! *A booty call.* At this moment, I also rehashed my automatic thoughts.

I am worthless.

I am insignificant.

I am nothing.

I'm only good for sex.

All the hard work I put into building my self-esteem and image for 20 years all went up in smoke in a matter of moments like the ill-fated World Trade Centers. Yes, that's how horrible I felt.

He wanted what others wanted, and I was no exception. The way men desired me and loved my presence; he watched from behind the scenes at every man who approached me and sparked up a conversation. I felt like he treated me like a dog at a fire hydrant to mark his territory. This made me think of how I felt when I was 13 when the boy threw pee in my face.

I was totally perplexed. How is it that his colleagues adored and appreciated and wanted me when I attended his conferences, but this man I secretly dated was shitting on me the entire time?

And that I allowed it.

"Why am I so worthless again?" Many nights I cried and didn't know how to get out of this.

You may say, "It's easy, Sarah, call him and say you're done with him. Or, don't call him at all." But for the life of me, I couldn't let him go. And surprisingly (or not) he wouldn't let me go.

Over the course of 2 years, neither one of us would let the other go. Neither one of us could pull away.

Until that fateful day.

I stopped talking to him for two months. During this time, I fasted 40 days and sought God's voice and direction for my life. My life was out of control, and I needed my Father's help. He answered. I had a major awakening and renewal. The milllonaire guy reached out to me to check in and invited me to meet up with him. *I declined!* OMG, I had enough strength to refuse. Shocked at my response, he left the invitation open anyway. I didn't take it. My power was coming back!

Until...

We agreed to meet at his home to discuss my business. Dammit, he knows how to get my attention.

My business was beginning to wane because I had very sporadic assistance for my parents' care, so I stepped away from my business to do 24/7 around the clock care for them. I didn't have any clients, and my reserves were almost depleted.

I made arrangements for my cousin to care for my parents while I went to his house. Upon arriving, he was busy packing for a trip. When he had time to talk about my business, I felt like he was putting down any and all of my ideas for reviving my business. Therefore, the nasty attacks on one another began.

I had so much pent up anger for this dude that it wasn't funny. I pushed all of his buttons, questioned his methods and intelligence, his leadership skills and his business strategies. I knew precisely how to assassinate his character. I began to hate him. I couldn't tell anyone of my dilemma, except my harem. But none of them were women so they just couldn't understand my headspace. I felt like I couldn't tell any of my girlfriends because of the mask I wore in front of them. None of them knew of this dark side of me. I was thoroughly ashamed.

Things took a turn for the worse. After repeated verbal attacks at one another, neither one of us saw what came next.

As he stood there drinking his wine with such a condescending look on his face, he asked me if there was anything else he could help me with. I took my right hand and smacked him clear across his face.

"And don't you ever call me a Bitch again."

Here is the context. He called me a bitch, to which I loathe. What I loathe the more is a total disregard for my request. I told him over the course of two years to NEVER call me a bitch. He felt that he used it as a compliment like, "You're a bad bitch."

He called me a bitch once again. I smacked him.

He then charged at me, banged me up against the wall and started choking me. He said, *"Don't you EVER Smack ME again! Don't you know people get killed for shit like that?"*

Time froze again.

It literally took me a moment to realize he was choking me and that I was struggling to breathe. *"Is this what you think of me? Is my life absolutely worthless to you that you would take it?"* Plenty of times I told him I meant nothing to him, and plenty of times he objected and told me he loves me.

This is love. To kill someone.

No one knew where I was. I never told anyone where I was going. I did not want to be a cold case, and I did not want to put my parents through losing their 2nd daughter. They already lost Michelle years ago, I couldn't have them lose me, too. I had a choice. Fight, flight, or freeze. Which response do you think I exhibited?

I mustered every bit of strength I had in my body, snatched his hands off of me pushed him across the room.

"Get the fuck off of me!" I yelled.

He comes back at me, grabs my arms put them behind my back and pins me down on his love seat.

"Didn't I tell you shit like that can get you killed?"

"Well, I did it, now what you gonna do about it?"

I was ready to take my 6-inch heel boots off and beat him with it. If I could just grab one of them! I dressed too cute for this occasion. I certainly wasn't ready for a fight that day. He easily pinned me down. But Lord knew that if I was about to check out of this earth, I wasn't checking out without a fight.

And I wasn't checking out alone.

He let me go and sat down. I got up off of the love seat, turned around and looked at him. I saw red and black and I felt it best to leave because I pictured cords and ropes that I could use on him. Additionally, I texted a couple of friends and told them who he was, what just happened, and his address if I wound up missing. If I didn't respond to my friends' texts in less than 24 hours, he would have been dead 24 hours later. That's a fact. "Sarah, don't you ever do something like that again! You don't go around putting your hands on people!"

"I don't put my hands on people, I put them on you!"

"For every action, there is a reaction, and I think you owe me an apology," he said.

"You tried to kill me."

"And you smacked me, by which I had incredible constraint. You ever heard of premeditated?"

"Wow, dude!"

I got my pocketbook and started to leave.

"Oh, you just going to leave" he said.

"Nigga, you put your hands on me one too many times."

"You smacked me."

"You called me a bitch."

"In a good way!"

"And you just choked me! I think I better leave!"

Here is the problem.

I didn't want to leave just as much as he didn't want me to leave. What in the world is going on? We sat and talked through this.

"I was trying to help you with your business, and this is the thanks I get?"

"You don't see anything wrong with you choking me? Trying to kill me?"

"You didn't expect a reaction after you smacked me?"

"What did I bruise?"

"My face is probably red."

"Here's the thing. You do not know me. I'm from Philly. The mean streets of North Philly. Don't let the doctorate or the clothes and fool you!"

"Why do Philly women fight? Women here are weak."

He acted like this was some drama show where the woman gets scared and recoils any ounce of power when the man throws his weight around and wraps his hand around her neck.

He had the wrong one.

We finished talking, and he said, "Don't you think you need to apologize?"

"I'm sorry," I said, as I snuggled up on him. "Now get into the bedroom!" We both chuckled. "Hey, it's your turn."

"Oh, it is? I'm sorry. Do you believe me?"

"The question is, do you believe me?"

He gave me the side eye for that one.

And back to business. He started giving me pointers on my business as he finished packing. I started heading for the door, to which he never likes when I start heading for the door and him not telling me when I can and cannot leave. I had to relieve my cousin from caring for my parents, so he walked me to the car. The decision was no more sex while he helps me with my business.

His thought was I reacted like a jilted girlfriend blinded by my love for him, and therefore we can no longer mix business and pleasure. He said that his only regret was mixing business with pleasure with me as opposed to maintaining a professional business relationship.

This fool. It had nothing to do with sex. It had to do with him lying to me. My automatic thoughts kicked up in full gear to defend myself against liars. He lost any intention for us to take this relationship to another level. I romanticized the idea of being a power couple instead of looking at what the entire relationship was, *Dominance and Control.*

I called my friend from Chester who would have killed him in 24 hours, and he told me why the guy reacted that way. *I bruised his ego.* This minion (me) had the gall to smack him. He thinks he is superior to all beings, and how dare I get in a position to smack the taste out of his mouth? The level of intensity in bruising his ego was equivalent to me being called a bitch. Except for me, being called a bitch didn't warrant death. Just a smack to bring him back down to earth. We were both wrong, and I could not fathom the varying degrees of our reactions, whereby my smacking him wouldn't have killed him. Him choking me could have killed me. I went to my parents' room, kissed my mom, thank God that I was alive, and then suddenly, it hit me.

I could have died. God told me two years before that if I stay with him, he will kill me.

I believe God spared me that day. I didn't adhere to what God put in my spirit. Never again will I disregard His Voice. Have you ever had those instances where you had a gut feeling not to do something but did it anyway, and it was costly? We need to respect our inner knowing and trust our gut. It never lies.

I reached out to him one time after that fateful day and another time to talk business. But after that, I realized I could not have any further involvement with him. Why?

Because of you.

I felt it was my duty to walk and maintain integrity, dignity, and respect for both myself and you. I am setting examples, and it would be hypocritical for me to tell you what not to do and I do it. My entire being just wouldn't allow me to be with him any longer.

The end.

I questioned my reactions to the whole encounter. When Anita Hill's actions were questioned as to why she continued to be in contact with Clarence Thomas, I thought that my actions would be questioned also. I couldn't use my counseling skills to figure out how I exhibited such behavior to support the argument regarding my worth. If I had worth, I would have left, or stop dealing with him. What went wrong? I put more value on what I could gain through him than on my own value system. Now that I was aware of my stinkin' thinkin', I was obligated to change it. It didn't go away by time; it goes away by taking ownership of my actions and not play the victim. I accurately place accountability on his part, but I had to look at myself and how I ended up being in this situation so that history doesn't repeat itself.

It does start with us, not with them.

I gladly take on the responsibility of sharing my voice so that you too know you have something bigger, beautiful and beyond you. You don't have time to play games. You don't have time to stay stuck. You don't have time to die in the mess that you've experienced. Use it to your advantage, build your strength, build your courage, and build your confidence. Build your voice.

Your voice is amazing; it has purpose, it has meaning, it has value, it has importance. That's the reframe. It's time for your rebirth. It's time for you to get out there and share your voice with the world. They are waiting for you!

My desire is for you to be a great contributor to this world to make it a better place. I can't do it alone. Many of us are speaking our voices, but we can't do it alone. We need you. You're the missing piece of the puzzle. Together, we can soar, rise and shine together.

I would like for you to join my Speak Your Voice Initiative. Spread the word and share your voices with others for gender equality. It's time for us to call it out and do something different to get different results.

This is the best time ever to do it!

SPEAK YOUR VOICE

Please join me in sharing your voice because it is our responsibility.

THE REVELATION
TIPS AND RECOMMENDATIONS

In order to get in position to share our voices, please do the following:

- ✓ **Don't look back.** I got out and never looked back because there is something bigger, beautiful and beyond me, which is you. I needed to get in formation to help you share your voice, speak your voice, give your voice, own your voice, show your voice, love your voice, hear your voice, build your voice, get your voice, find your voice, search your voice, and to be your voice. No looking back allowed other than to see how far you'd come.

- ✓ **Take responsibility**: I gladly took on the responsibility of sharing my voice so that you can also share yours. It is our duty and right to share our voices to make this world a better place for all to live in. We are our sister's and brother's keeper.

- ✓ **Believe in yourself**: You can do this! You will do this! You have been chosen and given every provision possible to win at life and succeed. Everyone sees it; we are waiting for you to receive it!

- ✓ **Be determined to play your part**: Know the role and the part you play in this puzzle. Own your lane. Know your gifts and talents and how to use them to your advantage and the benefit of others. Be prepared to do great things. You are in position to share your voice with the entire world.

- ✓ **Cut it off.** Remember, you must prune away dead weight, distractions, and defeats. Carrying all of this around doesn't serve you. Even if you have been successful, even if you use it to prove your naysayers wrong, you may be operating at only 50%. How much more powerful and how bad you could be if you operated in your full self at 100%? World, look out!!!

Spread the word about the Speak Your Voice Initiative and share your voices with others so that as a sisterhood brotherhood, humanhood, we can stand and fight for the same cause, movement, and revolution for change and gender equality. Now is the time for you to take your turn and ***Speak Your Voice.***

Speak Your Voice.

SPEAK YOUR VOICE

SELF REFLECTION EXERCISE

To **SHARE** Your Voice, get into a quiet space, and give yourself 15-30 minutes to do this exercise. Reflect, free associate, and write down your first thoughts that come to mind when answering the questions below without questioning or altering your answers.

What ways are you willing to share your voice? Who is your target audience?

_____
_____
_____

How will you start sharing your voice, i.e. blog, podcast, in person, etc.?

_____
_____
_____

What has held you back from sharing your voice? Why?

_____
_____
_____

What will you do differently to ensure you share your voice without anything holding you back this time?

_____
_____
_____

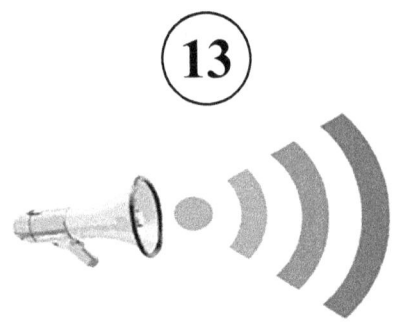

13

SELL YOUR VOICE

ROCK YOUR VOICE

It is yours after all.

"Making money is a hobby that will complement any other hobbies you have, beautifully."

– SCOTT ALEXANDER.

YOUR NARRATIVE

You have a story to tell. You have plenty of material to use to speak your voice about it. Do you know there are people out there who see you as a solution to their problems? They are even willing to pay you top dollar for your message and your story for the outcome they will experience because of you speaking your voice. Why not sell your voice? Why not monetize and leverage your voice? Do you know what monetize and leverage mean?

I created this bonus chapter just for you to learn how you can turn your story into impact and profit.

THE EDUCATION
HOW TO SELL YOUR STORY
What does monetize and leverage mean?

To monetize means to convert something to money. In economic terms, it is defined as converting any object or event, your own story in this case, into a form of currency with transferable value. Simply put, it's you earning money from telling your story.

Leverage, on the other hand, is the ability to influence an environment or a system in such a way that the result of one's effort will be multiplied to give more than the energy would deserve. In other words, it is the condition of reaping a relatively high level of returns from a relatively small effort or amount of cost. Putting in just enough effort and reaping so bountifully is the name of the game.

MAKING MILLIONS WITH YOUR STORY

Find your story: There is an opportunity to sell your story based on what you have gone through, which I call your life lessons. Your life lessons are what millions are waiting to obtain from you. Those millions are ready and willing to pay you for it. Therefore, the first step in leveraging your story is finding that story.

Your pain could be your purpose. Your frustration could be an opportunity to reach others. Your mess can become your message to empower other people.

Do not discard your life lessons; show your scar to others to empower them to show theirs. Remember, scars aren't bad. *Scars mean they are healed.*

Choose your audience: When you plan to monetize your message, one thing you want to be sure of is you want to attract the right people, which is called your *target audience.* Who are the people that will resonate with your story? Who are the people that your story is meant to influence and help? Be specific on who your message is for when it is time to sell your voice to them.

Have a compelling story: Your story has to be compelling and engaging to your audience. What habits are holding your audience back from success and how can you help them overcome it? What other challenges do you think might be confronting them and how can you solve it for them? It is not enough to give them more reasons to be angry with their situation without a way out, and that way out is what makes your story utterly compelling. Ask yourself how can you put together your experiences into a compelling narrative with conversations that will grab their attention, cause their emotions to erupt and most importantly, empower them to take action. *Remember, facts tell, but stories sell.* And the more funny you are, the more money they will spend on you.

Build a Platform: Next, you have to build a platform that you will be recognized for, share content consistently so you can build trust with your audience, and also position yourself as an expert or influencer Create a variety of content you can always share with them, just be sure that whenever they come, they will not be disappointed. Remember, think value for them by being valuable yourself.

Do you know you can speak your voice not only from a stage but by way of a digital product? This could come in several styles which would, in fact, form the basis of our next discussion. It is when you do this that the money begins to generate and you get paid just for telling your story and impacting lives.

THE CONVERSATION
LIFE LESSONS

I had learned how to sell my voice by way of a program, product, or service, and you can, too. If you are an introvert or too shy to publically speak, have no fear. There are plenty of ways to share your message and story with the world. Here are a few

- ✓ **Write a book:** Just like I am doing now and what countless others have done, you can sit down and put your life lessons to print as a how to guide for others. You can offer tips on how to go from victim to victor just like you. Your book is your glorified business card that you can monetize and leverage to convert prospects into clients and cash.

- ✓ **Be a coach:** Not only sports teams need coaches, but individuals also do too. We all need people who have been through what we are going through to guide us in making life decisions. One thing is sure, with a good coach in your life, you are in a better position to make excellent and much-informed choices and decisions compared to when you do not have a coach. You may choose to have a coaching business where you specialize in helping people with specific difficulties. This is an excellent way to launch your story and build credibility.

- ✓ **Do a podcast.** Take your voice to the airwaves or internet waves. You can share your stories by sound bites for those people who need to take you on the go. Your audience can download and listen to your podcast while jogging or driving to work. Why not share your life lessons by way of podcasting so that you can further your message to the masses?

- ✓ **Speaking engagement**: Introverts, look at this as an option (smile). Challenge yourself to speak to a crowd, and it can be small or as big as you want it. The point is using this platform as another avenue to further your message and expand your reach. Just consider. It is one of the top five money generating avenues.

- ✓ **Build Strategic Partnerships:** No man is an island; you can learn so much from others and establish relationships. Target those who are doing what you intend to do, listen to them speak, meet other people who have the same hunger as yours. Collaborate and form strategic partnerships that perhaps you can leverage and monetize in doing speaking engagements together and splitting the responsibilities and revenue down the middle. Now that's a win win win!

THE REVELATION
TIPS AND RECOMMENDATIONS

There are several ways I have learned in the course of my 20 years in business that can significantly improve your chance of success, particularly in selling your voice. One of which is by aligning your internal drives with your external goals, and to do that, here are my final 3 key components to consider:

Passion is that fuel that lights your creative path, it is that thing within you that grants you the competitive advantage that you can leverage every single day. It gives you an endless supply of energy from where it gives you the power to grow your business. Therefore, share your story with passion. Your story has to convince and compel you first before it will anyone else.

Purpose is is that thing you feel proud of, that thing you can commit your entire life to. Your purpose is the problem you are solving for your customers or the challenges you intend to help them with. Make sure that you are in alignment with your purpose both personally and professionally. It makes life that much more rewarding.

Profit is the result of a healthy, well-managed business. It is that which allows you to fund your venture and grants security and a healthy bank account. It is what you get from all your creativity, passion and purpose combined. While impact is the priority, profit is certainly next in line.

SPEAK YOUR VOICE
SELF REFLECTION EXERCISE

To **SELL** Your Voice, get into a quiet space, and give yourself 15-30 minutes to do this exercise. Reflect, free associate, and write down your first thoughts that come to mind when answering the questions below without questioning or altering your answers.

What is the problem that you solve for those who have experienced similar problems like you have experienced?

_____
_____
_____

Who is your target audience? Be specific. Age range, gender, occupation, socioeconomic status, location, ethnicity, etc.

_____
_____
_____

What is your message, or the solution or outcome that you bring to them?

_____
_____
_____

How will you spread your message to your audience in 30 days? What is your step by step plan of action?

_____
_____
_____

CONCLUSION

You have a story to tell, and your story matters. The value and relevancy of your story is not determined by what you think of your story, but by what others think of your story, especially the ones who need it.

Speak Your Voice. Your Story Matters. Your Voice Matters. Your Message Matters. It is an excellent time to start. Don't wait until you think you have it all together because really, no one has it all together. We are all imperfectly perfect.

You Speak Your Voice for impact. Stimulate revelation conversation and education. Keep in mind that your voice is for someone's breakthrough, transformation and shift.

Speak Your Voice for value. Focus on how to add value to the lives you touch. Share your life lessons. Give them tips and recommendations on how to speak their voices. Reframe their mindsets. Be the example.

Lastly, Speak Your Voice For Yourself. This is your defining moment. This is for your healing and breakthrough. To dare challenge any self-doubt that what you say or who you are equate relevance. You are relevant and bring much to the table for the entire world. You are worth Speaking Your Voice.

I thank you for allowing me to speak my voice to you, and for allowing me to simply be me. If you need me, I am here for you.

You are now ready to Speak Your Voice.

AFTERWORD

I had the pleasure of meeting Dr. Sarah Langley more than a year ago. It was an encounter that I know was God designed. We were both attending a women's conference and were there for different reasons. Sarah was there as the keynote speaker, and I was there doing media coverage and Red-carpet interviews. When Sarah came into the room, I immediately connected with her before she ever said a word. She looked as if she was there on a mission and let me tell you that looks are not deceiving. I remember thinking, wow she appears to be so confident and I soon found out that it wasn't an appearance it was really who she was. We ended up in the bathroom at the same time where the connection I felt was indeed confirmed. Sarah calls it a meeting in the lady's room, and I will agree that it was. It was a meeting of the minds. We spoke of our perspective organizations and initiatives. We found that our passion to see individuals set free from trauma and set back were literally the same, and we both had a focus on young girls and women we knew that God was up to something. Dr. Sarah Renee Langley's book *Speak Your Voice* is an amazing read that will help you get your power, your confidence, and the ability, strength to unmute your voice. As the founder and President of LeadHer International, LLC Dr. Sarah Renee Langley has coached and helped countless individuals to reach goals that seemed unattainable through reframing the way you think, reprioritizing and reinventing your life. Speak Your Voice is not just a movement it is indeed a way of life. I am honored to not only know her but to come alongside her, to stand in the gap for those who have yet to find, discover and speak their voice. As the Founder and CEO of Kingdom Women Rock Outreach Ministries, Author of Damaged 2 Delivered "Finding Joy On the Journey" I can attest to the difficulty and the opposition that comes as a result of standing in your truth and Speaking Your Voice. However, I do believe in the power that Speak Your Voice will give you as you apply all the nuggets shared in this book to your life. Watch how free you will then become because of the sacrifice and obedience Dr. Sarah Renee Langley applied to deliver every word that is shared in this book to the world at large.

Joyce Lester AKA Lady Joy

SPECIAL THANKS

Special Thanks to Ms. Tarana Burke for creating #Metoo in 2006 before it was a hashtag.

"Me Too"

Special Thanks to Ms. Anita Hill for having the courage to #speakyourvoice so that I can speak my voice today.

"Speak Your Voice Now"

RESOURCE: ROCK YOUR VOICE

Are you ready to Rock Your Voice? After learning the secrets of Speaking Your Voice, and receiving my bonus chapter, Sell Your Voice, I want to position you to Rock Your Voice.

What is Rock Your Voice? It is my signature speaker coaching program guaranteed to build your signature speech, brand, and audience for massive profits. If you are interested in having a deeper conversation and learning the fundamentals of Rocking Your Voice for purpose, power, and profit, go to my scheduler https://my.timetrade.com/book/1Q4GP

And book your call to get one step closer to #RockYourVoice.

Go to drsarahreneelangley.com to check out my other products and services and events happening near you.

Here is one of my resources: 5 Easy Steps to Building Your Message For Millions as a Professional Speaker.

Enjoy.

BUILD YOUR MESSAGE FOR MILLIONS

STEP 1: BE THE EXPERT

How do you become an expert? Let us describe what an expert is. The term 'expert' is used to describe a person with significant life experience or academic training in a particular field. We all have compelling life experiences, but not all of us evaluate those experiences into life lessons that could, in fact, help others. To be a speaker, you need to assess your life lessons to determine if the information you share is beneficial and valuable to your audience. You can always share similar life stories like family and relationships, overcoming an addiction or assault, handling racial issues and abuses, and positive personal growth.

STEP 2: DEVELOP YOUR SKILLS

Some are natural born speakers. However, if you do not possess strong public speaking skills, you can always take formal classes. From universities to speaking organizations, you can learn how to deliver persuasive speeches, incorporate body language, use technology, field audience questions, and much more. Additionally, you can test the waters by engaging your audience through practicing on social media. Facebook Lives and Podcasts are great ways to develop your skills organically. Find opportunities to speak, whether at your job, through

Toastmasters, or at a friend's birthday party. You name it, use any and every opportunity possible to build and practice your skills as a professional speaker.

STEP 3: BUILD THE EXPERIENCE

There is speaking and there is professional speaking. You would need the experience to get to higher levels and to do this, you may need to volunteer to speak at local events, schools, charitable organizations, or community centers. You need real-world experiences to develop your style and presentation as that would serve you well in the long run. Don't forget to garner testimonials to build credibility with your audience.

STEP 4: MAKE YOUR STORY UNIQUE

Everyone has a unique story, but not everyone knows how to use their story to set themselves apart from their competitor. You must take time to create services that will bring better results than others. Study those who are doing what you are doing. Also, study your competitors and see what they are not doing. Use that opportunity to fill in the gap that you see happening in your marketplace and build your story around that. Think and position yourself to be the solution to your audience's problem through your story. Facts tell. Stories sell.

STEP 5: GET PAID TO SPEAK

Once you have put enough public speaking tips and techniques to use during your free speeches, you are ready to get paid. Eventually, some people will enjoy your speech so much that you will begin to hear things like "How much would you charge to give that talk to the people in my group." That is the starting point of your career and so be sure not to sell yourself short.

.

Speak your voice.
The world awaits you.

ABOUT THE AUTHOR

An Award Winning International Speaker, Executive Leadership Coach, Mentor and Author, **Dr. Sarah Renee Langley** is the go to expert who has proven to captivate her audience and take the entire team or individual to their next level. Highly sought after, Dr. Langley's features include but are not limited to, ABC, Fox News, CBS News and Good Morning America. As the CEO and Founder of Leadher International Dr. Langley stands ready to execute her mission to mobilize women leaders to tap into their limitless potentials and boldly unleash their greatness. Having traveled the world motivating women that are seeking to live a life filled with purpose, she is the investment that is sure to render a significant return. Being a successful woman in a corporate world founded and dominated by men, Dr. Sarah Renee Langley's experiences have afforded her the chance to develop effective strategies to overcome an array of obstacles and become a part of the great shift. She proves time and time again how core principles, values and beliefs determine predictable outcomes. Her counseling experience coupled with superb leadership skills allows her to engage listeners, educate clients and equip them with substantial strategies to compete on their next level. Ready to connect with the team, group or individual, Dr. Langley will identify barriers and offer substantial solutions that will direct everyone's focus toward endless possibilities. Schedule a meeting Dr. Sarah and be the next to advance forward in your professional position and/or life.